Tony & Chris Groom

Dales
Rail Trails

2020
Published by Skyware Ltd.

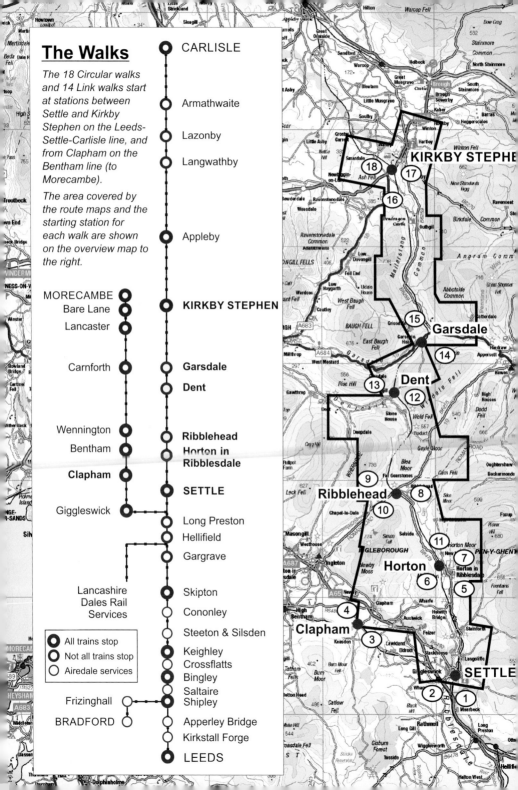

The Walks

The 18 Circular walks and 14 Link walks start at stations between Settle and Kirkby Stephen on the Leeds-Settle-Carlisle line, and from Clapham on the Bentham line (to Morecambe).

The area covered by the route maps and the starting station for each walk are shown on the overview map to the right.

CARLISLE

Armathwaite

Lazonby

Langwathby

Appleby

KIRKBY STEPHEN

Garsdale

Dent

Ribblehead

Horton in Ribblesdale

SETTLE

Long Preston

Hellifield

Gargrave

Skipton

Cononley

Steeton & Silsden

Keighley

Crossflatts

Bingley

Saltaire

Shipley

Apperley Bridge

Kirkstall Forge

LEEDS

MORECAMBE
Bare Lane
Lancaster

Carnforth

Wennington
Bentham

Clapham

Giggleswick

Lancashire Dales Rail Services

Frizinghall

BRADFORD

- ◉ All trains stop
- ◉ Not all trains stop
- ○ Airedale services

CIRCULAR WALKS

LINEAR LINK WALKS

INTRODUCTION

The Yorkshire Dales offer some of the finest walking in England. In an area of less than a thousand square miles you will find a unique blend of contrasting landscapes.

Gleaming white limestone terraces carpeted in well-drained, springy turf are a delight to walk on. Climb higher and the steep rocky peaks, sometimes clouded in mist and battered by rain, prove a worthy challenge. You will find peace and solitude on the wild, lonely heather-clad moorlands, whilst the broad green valleys, fed by sparkling streams and dramatic waterfalls, are a pleasure to explore.

The Yorkshire Dales are carved from the mid Pennines, the mountainous backbone of England. Deep valleys, the dales, are cut into high rolling hills – the fells. Streams, or becks, gather on the hill tops to begin their long journey to the sea.

The broad valleys are scattered with stone farmsteads and barns, criss-crossed by miles of dry stone walls. The tiny Dales villages give a warm welcome to visitors, and the remote Dales inns, which for centuries have provided a refuge for packhorse traders and drovers, now offer the same to walkers.

Running right across the heart of the western Dales is England's most beautiful railway, the Settle to Carlisle line, recently voted one of the finest railway journeys in the world. What better way to explore the Dales?

You can travel from Leeds or Carlisle in little over an hour, giving plenty of time for a full day's walk, perhaps enjoying a pint or two before catching the return train home.

Better still, why not take an overnight stay along the line and enjoy two full days' walking? If you're coming from further afield, then the market towns of Settle to the south or Kirkby Stephen to the north make a great base for a walking holiday, using the train to explore the entire length of the Dales.

There is also an extensive bus network – DalesBus – which allows walks to be extended across the Dales. You can, of course, arrive by car, perhaps using the train to return on the linear routes. If so, you should use the car parks provided and be prepared to pay towards their upkeep.

This book includes 18 circular walks from stations between Settle and Kirkby Stephen, each between 6 and 13 miles long, with detailed maps and notes. The walks can also be linked together, giving 14 linear walks from station to station. Taken as a whole they provide comprehensive coverage of the area of the western Dales along the railway and will give a good overall appreciation and understanding of the landscape.

Generally the routes stick to rights of way, or follow fairly well-trod paths over Open Access land. In two cases, around Kirkby Stephen, they make use of permissive routes where access could, in the future, be removed.

The book includes details of the Yorkshire Three Peaks Challenge route – a tough but popular walk of 24 miles taking in Pen-y-ghent, Whernside and Ingleborough. For the lover of long-distance walking, there's also the Six Peaks Trail - a 48-mile high-level route from Settle to Kirkby Stephen, following the railway line.

Finally, there is a lot of additional information available on the website, including details of any route updates, timetables, accommodation and other facilities along the way, plus outlines of additional walks. Go to **www.dalesrailtrails.co.uk**

(Above) Catrigg Force, Stainforth
(Below) Walkers above Hangingstone Scar, Mallerstang
(Opposite) Climbing from Dentdale on the Craven Way

7

How to use this book

There are three things you will need to get the most from this book:

1) A reasonable level of fitness: all the walks cover at least six miles and involve some uphill walking.

2) An ability to read a simple map: the main route descriptions take the form of a map, with additional helpful notes. The text alone is not sufficient for navigation.

3) Decent walking kit: good boots, waterproofs, a fleece and hat – the upper fells are very exposed and conditions can quickly turn wet and cold, even in summer.

The routes are graded for the effort required:

EASY walks are up to 8 miles in length and may involve an overall ascent of 400 metres;

MODERATE walks are from 8 to 10 miles long or include an ascent of between 400 and 500 metres;

STRENUOUS walks are at least 10 miles long or include total ascent of more than 500 metres.

You should start off with a couple of EASY walks first to get a feel for them. It will also give you some idea of how your normal pace relates to the timings that are given. These are for guidance only and don't include any time for stops or breaks; you will need to add

those in. The timings are based on a walking rate of 2½ miles an hour, with an additional hour for every 600 metres of ascent.

Half-way points along the main circular routes are shown on the maps, to help you judge progress. Some walks include optional shortcuts or diversions. Some may also include suggestions for extensions which are not included on the maps – you will need the appropriate OS map for these.

All the routes in this book are covered by just two OS Explorer maps – OL2 & OL19 – the best maps for walkers at a scale of 1:25,000. It is advisable to carry the appropriate OS map with you, with a compass and/or a GPS.

The maps in this book are shown at the same 1:25,000 scale and are based on these OS maps, but with superfluous detail omitted. All the routes have been surveyed on the ground prior to publication, but you should always bear in mind that the countryside changes – new fences appear; stiles are replaced by gates; signs disappear.

We are very fortunate in this country to have an extensive network of public footpaths and bridleways – rights of way – there for all to enjoy. Many upland areas are also designated Open Access land where you generally have the right to roam. These hard-won freedoms should be enjoyed responsibly.

Gates or gateways are marked with a **g** on the maps. Those which provide sole access on rights of way should be unlocked; those on Open Access land where there is no right of way, but where you enjoy the *right to roam* may be locked. Here you are permitted to climb a locked gate, providing you cause no damage.

A stile is indicated by an **s** on a map, as is a stile and gate together, in which case you may prefer to use the gate. Where the two are close by on a right of way, the gate may sometimes be locked.

If you're walking one of the link routes, starting and finishing at a different station, you should buy a return ticket to the furthest station. If the stations are on different lines – such as *Link Walk L3* from Clapham to Settle - then again buy a return ticket to the furthest station (Clapham in this case), but be prepared to buy a further single ticket on the train between the other station (Settle) and the nearest common junction (Hellifield or Long Preston). The conductors on these trains are generally pretty relaxed, so with luck they'll let you off.

All the routes in this book, almost in their entirety, fall within the area of the Yorkshire Dales National Park (short sections at Settle and Kirkby Stephen fall outside). The condition of the footpaths - waymarking, stiles, footbridges etc. is therefore generally very good.

A day pack is useful. You will need to carry plenty to drink – enough for a full day – and food. Some of the walks, particularly as you move north, cover remote areas with few facilities. Consider carrying a walking pole, even if you don't normally use one – it can help crossing wet or boggy ground; on steep, rocky descents; or if you're unlucky enough to twist an ankle or knee.

Carrying a mobile phone might be useful in an EMERGENCY, though you may well lose a signal altogether on the remote fells. If you do get into difficulty, at the first opportunity call 999 and ask for the POLICE, then tell the police you need MOUNTAIN RESCUE.

In any case you should avoid the higher fells altogether in misty or icy conditions. Be prepared to turn around if conditions deteriorate - you can always come back another time. IF IN DOUBT, TURN ABOUT.

A dog can be a great companion on a walk, but should be kept under control at all times, and put on a short lead if there's livestock about or on the open fells from March to July when ground birds are nesting. Dogs are not allowed on some Open Access areas.

There have been some tragic incidents where dog walkers have been injured or killed by cattle. Cows can be particularly protective of young calves, so give these a wide berth and keep your dog on a short lead. If you do get into trouble, let the dog go – it can outrun cattle. Get yourself to safety then call the dog back.

Tread lightly and take your rubbish home. As the saying goes: *take only photographs, leave only footprints*.

Summer meadow in Ribblesdale.
(Opposite) Ingleborough from Twistleton.

The Leander - a steam charter at Birkett Common, Mallerstang (above)
A diesel Sprinter pulls into Ribblehead Station (below)   (Photos © Pete Shaw)

The Settle-Carlisle Railway

The Settle to Carlisle Railway has been voted amongst the top train journeys in the world, and not without good reason. The scenic views, particularly between Settle and Appleby, are fabulous – made even more so if you are returning from a walk across that very landscape.

Although weekly steam charters are a favourite feature of the railway throughout the summer, attracting hordes of photographers along the line, the regular mainline services are provided by speedy diesel Sprinters.

The line itself actually runs between Leeds and Carlisle, but the section from Settle was built to provide the Midland Railway Company with its own connection between London and Scotland. The building of the line began in 1869 and was the last of the great Victorian construction projects, built largely by hand with 6,000 men working on the project at its peak. Scheduled to take just four years, it actually took seven to complete.

In 1963 the Beeching Report condemned the line as uneconomic and the service was run down, so that by the 1970s only Appleby station was open between Settle and Carlisle, and just two trains ran each day.

In 1974 the West Riding Ramblers Association organised a walkers' charter train, which was such a great success it was taken up by the National Park Authority. Weekend Dales Rail charter trains stopped at the then near derelict stations at Horton-in-Ribblesdale, Ribblehead, Dent, Garsdale and Kirkby Stephen. The Friends of DalesRail (FDR) was formed to organise guided walks from the line.

Finally in 1983 British Rail announced that they wished to close the line. By this time the Friends of the Settle-Carlisle Line (FoSCL) had already been formed to campaign against the threatened closure, and campaign they did!

The Public Hearings into the proposed closure brought a record number of objectors – 22,265 people and one dog. Ruswarp, the faithful companion of FoSCL secretary Graham Nuttall was accepted as a bona fide fare paying rail user (a bronze statue of Ruswarp can be seen at Garsdale Station, and the incredible story of his loyalty can be read inside the waiting room).

On 11 April 1989, transport secretary Michael Portillo finally announced the line's reprieve. Speaking about the campaign years later as he travelled the line again on BBC television, Portillo, a railway enthusiast, admitted that saving the Settle Carlisle was his greatest achievement in politics.

"As I think back on it, two decades later, the moment I took up my pen and signed the reprieve is one of the happiest days of my political career. The Settle to Carlisle railway line was saved."

FoSCL now had to re-invent itself as a user and support group, to improve facilities and services for passengers. With over 3,000 members, it is probably the largest rail support group in the UK. Volunteers have helped refurbish and maintain station buildings and disused signal boxes and run regular on-train guide services.

Both FoSCL and FDR also run a programme of free led walks from train stations along the line, covering all the routes in this book and many more besides. Their members also help organise the annual *Ride2Stride Walking Festival*.

Their walk programmes can be found in the stations, or online, and for those who enjoy good company and the guidance of an experienced walk leader, there's no better way to utilise the train for exploring the surrounding landscape.

Graham Nuttall and Ruswarp
(Photo: © Sunday Mirror)

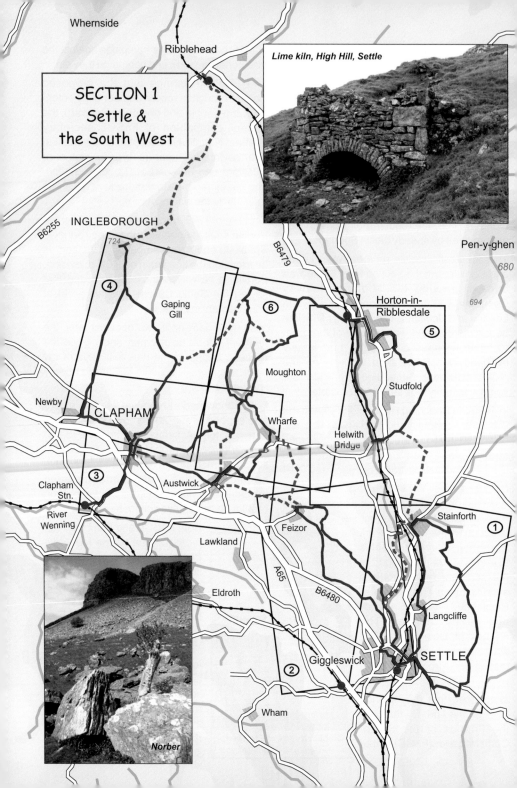

Whernside

Ribblehead

SECTION 1
Settle &
the South West

Lime kiln, High Hill, Settle

B6255

INGLEBOROUGH

724

Pen-y-ghen

680

B6479

④

Gaping
Gill

⑥

Horton-in-
Ribblesdale

694

⑤

Moughton

Studfold

Newby

CLAPHAM

Wharfe

Helwith
Bridge

③

Austwick

Clapham
Stn.

River
Wenning

Stainforth

①

Feizor

Lawkland

A65

B6480

Langcliffe

Eldroth

SETTLE

②

Giggleswick

Wham

Norber

SECTION ONE: Settle & the South West

North of Settle is beautiful limestone country, which perhaps gives the Yorkshire Dales its most unique character. The limestone rises suddenly from the gritstone moorland to the south along a series of natural fractures in the earth's crust known as the Craven Faults. One fracture runs northwest from Settle, along the route of the A65, showing itself in the steep escarpment of Giggleswick Scar.

Limestone produces well drained, springy turf which is a real pleasure to walk on. Here you will find the largest outcropping of limestone in the country, a treasure of brilliant white cliffs, screes, pavements, potholes and caves. Like all the rocks of the Dales, the thick layers of Great Scar Limestone, almost pure calcium carbonate, are sedimentary in nature. They sit in horizontal layers on top of the much older, harder basement rocks, whose beds have been tilted and folded by tectonic forces.

The area is rich in archaeology. There is evidence that the first hardy humans to set foot here may have made their way from the continent into the frozen tundra 14,000 years ago, during a brief warmer spell towards the end of the last Ice Age. Carved antler rods found in Victoria Cave, near Settle, have been dated to the late Paleolithic.

The walks in this section cover the area of the south-western Dales between Settle and Horton-in-Ribblesdale in the north, and Clapham in the west. The walks are mostly shorter and easier than others in the book and the going underfoot is generally good. There's plenty of variety and interest, great views and some fine challenges. You're also never very far from a settlement where refreshment might be found, so these are good walks to start with. Austwick, Stainforth and Helwith Bridge, for example, have pubs although they are not necessarily open all day and Elaine's Tearoom at Feizor is a real walkers' favourite.

Settle is the gateway to the western Dales. This lovely Dales market town makes the perfect base for a walking holiday and has everything you might need, including cafes, shops, banks, supermarkets, a library and a museum. There's plenty of accommodation and several good pubs. The station is close to the town centre and is the model of how everyone thinks a small town railway station should be, thanks in no small part to the volunteers who help look after it.

The town is Anglian in origin, dating from the 7th century, but following the Norman conquest in 1066 and the bloody *Harrying of the North* that followed, Settle was subsequently described as *waste* in the Domesday book. The town recovered and in 1249 was granted its market charter.

Across the river from Settle is the ancient Norse settlement of Giggleswick, best known today for its public school, founded in 1507, with its copper-domed chapel. The prosperous little village was the site of the Astronomer Royal's expedition in 1924 to view the solar eclipse. Giggleswick Station is on the Bentham line, half a mile from the village, and a mile from Settle Station, with the Craven Arms Hotel just opposite.

The railway forks south of Settle, with the Settle-Carlisle line running north and the Bentham line bearing west to Morecambe, passing through Giggleswick and Clapham. The most useful junction station is Hellifield, with its tea shop, where most trains stop.

Clapham Station is just over a mile south west of the village it serves, linked by a quiet country road. Clapham itself, now bypassed by the busy A65, is a beautiful village stretched out alongside Clapham Beck. With its shops, café bars, accommodation and the New Inn Hotel it makes a tranquil base for a walking holiday. Ingleborough Hall, former home of the Farrer family, is now an outdoor centre, and the estate can be explored along a nature trail, leading to the famous Ingleborough Show Cave. It is also the starting point for perhaps the finest ascent of Ingleborough peak.

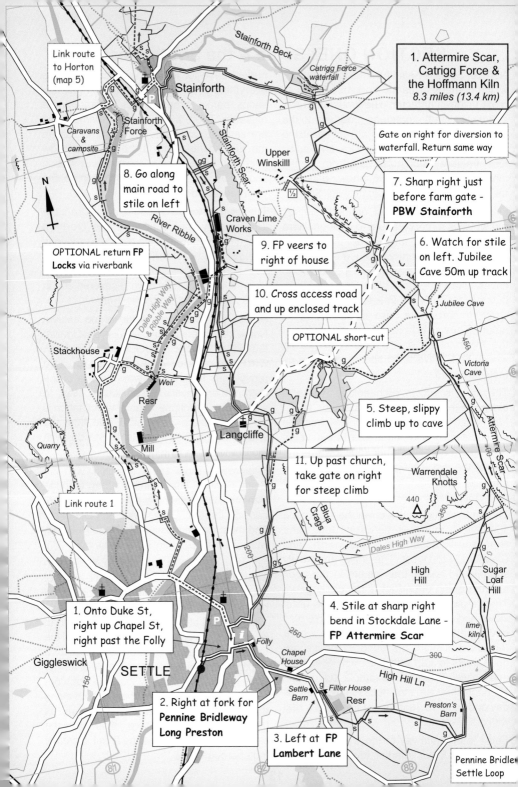

Link route to Horton (map 5)

Stainforth Beck

Catrigg Force waterfall

Stainforth

1. Attermire Scar, Catrigg Force & the Hoffmann Kiln
8.3 miles (13.4 km)

Caravans & campsite

Stainforth Force

Upper Winskilll

Gate on right for diversion to waterfall. Return same way

8. Go along main road to stile on left

N

River Ribble

Stainforth Scar

½

7. Sharp right just before farm gate - PBW Stainforth

Craven Lime Works

9. FP veers to right of house

6. Watch for stile on left. Jubilee Cave 50m up track

OPTIONAL return **FP Locks** via riverbank

Dales High Way & Ribble Way

10. Cross access road and up enclosed track

3 Jubilee Cave

OPTIONAL short-cut

Victoria Cave

Stackhouse

450

Weir

Resr

5. Steep, slippy climb up to cave

Attermire Scar

Quarry

Mill

Langcliffe

11. Up past church, take gate on right for steep climb

Warrendale Knotts

440 △

Link route 1

Blue Crags

Dales High Way

High Hill

Sugar Loaf Hill

1. Onto Duke St, right up Chapel St, right past the Folly

Gigglewick

SETTLE

P

i

Folly

4. Stile at sharp right bend in Stockdale Lane - FP Attermire Scar

lime kiln

250

Chapel House

High Hill Ln

300

2. Right at fork for Pennine Bridleway Long Preston

Settle Barn

Filter House

Resr

Preston's Barn

3. Left at FP Lambert Lane

81

82

83

Pennine Bridleway Settle Loop

1. Attermire Scar, Catrigg Force & the Hoffmann Kiln

Settle   8.3 miles *(13.4 km)*   Time: 4:15   Ascent: 490m   *Moderate*

An excellent introduction to the limestone landscape of the Dales - scar, scree, cave and waterfall.

From Settle climb the narrow road up past the 17th century **Folly** and left along the road for **Kirkby Malham** (1). At the Chapel House fork right onto the old moor road to **Long Preston** (2). Climb steeply past the Filter House and reservoir, cross a stile and follow the track rising diagonally left to cross a wall stile on the right. Follow the wall on the left over several fields to reach **Lambert Lane**, which leads up to High Hill Lane and onto **Stockdale Lane** (3). A stile at a right bend for **Attermire Scar** (4) leads you rising on a broad green path into limestone country.

A small lime kiln on the hillside is one of 800 or so found across the Dales. Mostly dating from the 18th century onwards, they burnt locally quarried limestone to produce lime - used to sweeten the land for agriculture, or slaked with water for use in mortar or limewash.

Pass the conic Sugar Loaf Hill and drop to cross a wall stile, before climbing north between Warrendale Knotts and Attermire Scar, with **Victoria Cave** up on the right (5).

Excavated in the 1870s, the cave has produced a wealth of archaeological treasures, including an 11,000 year old bone harpoon point and the bone fragments of lion, elephant and hippopotamus.

Drop to a gate to join a clear track. Go right to a ladder stile on the wall on your left. Over this swing right and go on to join the road. Turn down the access road for Upper Winskill farm. Just before the farm gate turn right (7) and follow the clear track, swinging left to drop to an enclosed track for **Stainforth**. A gate on the right leads down to the spectacular **Catrigg Force**, best seen from the bottom where a scramble across slippery rocks is necessary. Return the same way.

Take the main road heading towards Settle (8). A wall stile on the left for **Langcliffe** leads across several fields beneath the white cliffs of Stainforth Scar to reach the site of Craven Lime Works and the huge **Hoffmann Kiln**.

Built in 1837 to meet industrial demand for lime, the kiln had 22 individual burning chambers built around a huge oval. Lime was produced in a continuous process, taking six weeks for one complete circuit. The kiln and its quarry ceased operating in 1931 due to falling demand and competition elsewhere. Now a scheduled monument, the National Park Authority has carried out conservation work and installed information boards to help you explore this fascinating site.

Beyond the kiln, veer to the right of a house alongside the railway on a narrow path (9). Cross the access road by the railway bridge (10) and up an enclosed track opposite for **Langcliffe** (or turn under the arch and cross the road for an easier riverside return). Follow the path rising across several fields to reach another enclosed track leading into the village. Climb up behind the church (11), along the bridleway for **Settle**, climbing steeply to follow the path above the walls, eventually joining an enclosed track to drop back into Settle via Constitution Hill.

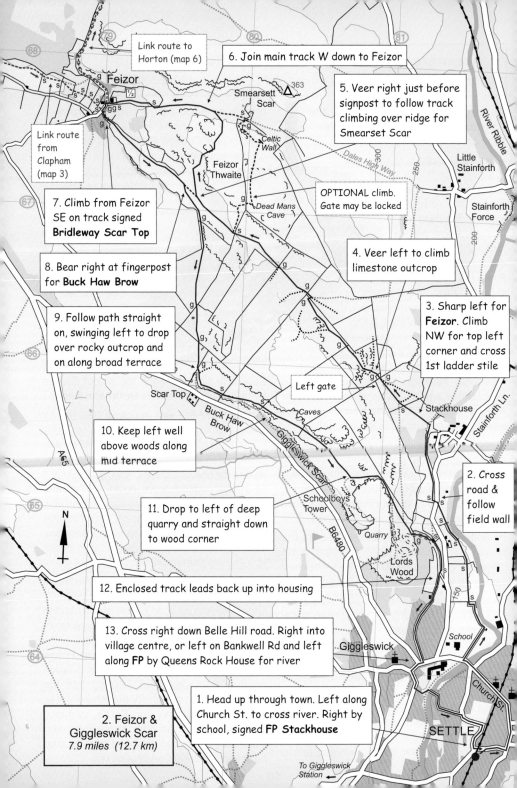

Link route to Horton (map 6)

6. Join main track W down to Feizor

5. Veer right just before signpost to follow track climbing over ridge for Smearset Scar

Feizor

Smearsett Scar △363

Celtic Wall

Dales High Way

Little Stainforth

Stainforth Force

Link route from Clapham (map 3)

Feizor Thwaite

Dead Mans Cave

OPTIONAL climb. Gate may be locked

7. Climb from Feizor SE on track signed **Bridleway Scar Top**

4. Veer left to climb limestone outcrop

8. Bear right at fingerpost for **Buck Haw Brow**

3. Sharp left for **Feizor**. Climb NW for top left corner and cross 1st ladder stile

9. Follow path straight on, swinging left to drop over rocky outcrop and on along broad terrace

Left gate

Stackhouse

Stainforth Ln.

Scar Top

Buck Haw Brow

Caves

2. Cross road & follow field wall

10. Keep left well above woods along mid terrace

Giggleswick Scar

Schoolboys Tower

11. Drop to left of deep quarry and straight down to wood corner

B6480

Quarry

Lords Wood

12. Enclosed track leads back up into housing

13. Cross right down Belle Hill road. Right into village centre, or left on Bankwell Rd and left along **FP** by Queens Rock House for river

Giggleswick

School

Church St.

2. Feizor & Giggleswick Scar
7.9 miles (12.7 km)

1. Head up through town. Left along Church St. to cross river. Right by school, signed **FP Stackhouse**

SETTLE

To Giggleswick Station ←

N

A65

2. Feizor & Giggleswick Scar

Settle   **7.9 miles** *(12.7 km)*   Time: **4:00**   Ascent: **390m**   *Easy*

A fine walk across gentle limestone hills to the tiny hamlet of Feizor, with a return along the dramatic scars of the South Craven Fault to Giggleswick.

From Settle town centre head north along Church Street and across the river Ribble. Turn right along a track between sports fields for **Stackhouse** and follow the clear path above the river to join Stainforth Lane (1).

Cross the road and a stile opposite (2) and follow the path right, alongside the wall towards Stackhouse, climbing behind the hamlet. Just beyond the woods turn sharp left for **Feizor** (3) to climb away from the hamlet, heading for the top left corner of the field. Cross the first of two ladder stiles and go up to and through the left of two gates. Beyond a second gate, veer left to climb over limestone outcrops (4), with fine views now of Pen-y-ghent. Curve right to a gate in a dog-legged wall corner and continue with the wall on your right as the path levels, heading north-west.

Continue straight on through several fields with Ingleborough coming into view ahead, finally descending to a ladder stile beside a gate. The path ahead drops straight to Feizor.

*An option here is to climb alongside the wall on the right to a gate onto Feizor Thwaite. Just beyond is **Dead Man's Cave**. Turn left and follow the track across the hill to reach the enigmatic **Celtic Wall**. Why and when it was built is unknown. Climb down at the left field corner to join the track, left, to Feizor.*

Otherwise, go down to a confluence of tracks by a fingerpost, turning right to follow a clear track climbing towards Smearsett Scar over Open Access land (5). Go straight on to follow the track down into the dry valley (6) below Smearsett Scar, swinging left down to Feizor.

Turn down the lane, then left along the bridleway for **Scar Top** (7). At the fingerpost turn right for **Buck Haw Brow** (8). Beyond a bridle gate, the clear track heads straight south, through three more gates with Pendle Hill ahead in the distance. The path finally swings left to drop over a rocky outcrop and follow a broad terrace above the scar, with fine views now across the Forest of Bowland.

Giggleswick Scar marks the line of the South Craven Fault, one of several fractures in the earth's crust here, where the limestone beds to the north have risen whilst those to the south have sunk and been subsequently covered with layers of shale and sandstone.

Easy walking now, keeping to the left at a fork (10), to pass a series of caves on the left and several cairns on the right, the biggest being the ruined **Schoolboys Tower**.

Follow the track marked with posts (11), to the top of a former limestone quarry, curving left down the north side along a clear track to a wall corner and through a gate along an access track in the woods. Cross the wall on the left for a short way. Ignore a left fork to the house and go along a rising enclosed track that leads onto a road - The Mains - past large houses and out onto the main road (12).

Go down the road opposite right - **Belle Hill**. At the bottom a right takes you along Church St. into the village centre of Giggleswick, otherwise turn left along Bankwell Rd (*Giggleswick Station is one mile further on*). Turn left through a narrow ginnel by Queens Rock House which leads to the river (13). Cross the river footbridge, following the signs for the town centre and the railway station.

The Celtic Wall

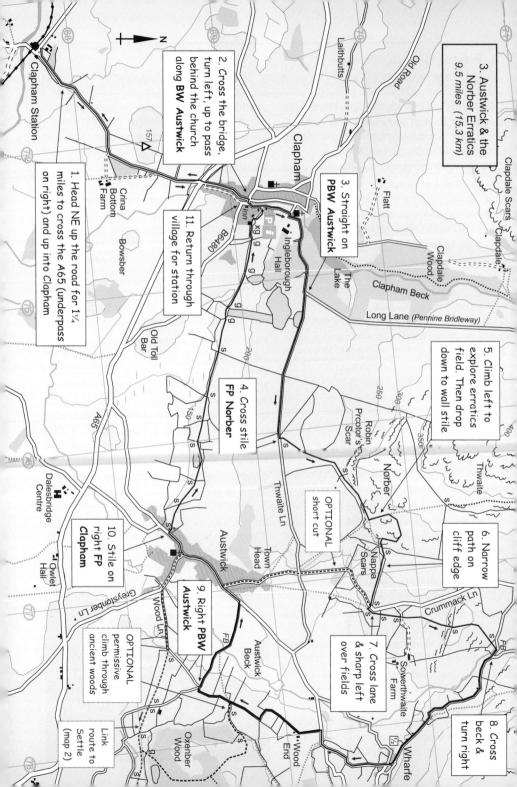

3. Austwick & the Norber Erratics
9.5 miles (15.3 km)

1. Head NE up the road for 1¼ miles to cross the A65 (underpass on right) and up into Clapham

2. Cross the bridge, turn left, up to pass behind the church along **BW Austwick**

3. Straight on **PBW Austwick**

4. Cross stile **FP Norber**

5. Climb left to explore erratics field. Then drop down to wall stile

6. Narrow path on cliff edge

7. Cross lane & sharp left over fields

8. Cross beck & turn right

9. Right **PBW Austwick**

10. Stile on right **FP Clapham**

11. Return through village for station

OPTIONAL short cut

OPTIONAL permissive climb through ancient woods

Link route to Settle (map 2)

Clapham Station

Clapham

Crina Bottom Farm

Bowsber

Ingleborough Hall

The Lake

Clapham Beck

Long Lane (Pennine Bridleway)

Laithbutts

Flatt

Clapdale Scars

Clapdale/

Old Road

Clapdale Wood

Robin Proctor's Scar

Norber

Thwaite

Thwaite Ln

Town Head

Nappa Scars

Crummack Ln

Sowerthwaite Farm

Wharfe

Wood End

Austwick Beck

Oxenber Wood

Austwick

Wood Ln

Greystonber Ln

Dalesbridge Centre

Owlet Hall

A65

Old Toll Bar

B6480

FB

157

200

250

300

350

450

3. Austwick & the Norber Erratics

Clapham **9.5 miles** *(15.3 km)* Time: **4:30** Ascent: **360m** *Moderate*

A fascinating walk exploring some of the geological treasures of the area around quiet, secluded Crummackdale. Graded easy but for the long walk from the station.

From the station walk NE up the road into Clapham (1). Cross the bridge and turn left up Church Ave to pass behind the church and up a stony track marked **BW Austwick** (2). The track climbs steeply through two tunnels and curves right before finally reaching a junction of ways as it levels out. Go straight on along the Pennine Bridleway for **Austwick** (3).

Thwaite Lane is part of an ancient route that connected Fountains Abbey with its many interests towards the west. It is an extension of Mastiles Lane from Wharfedale to Malham.

A stile on the left by a gate, **FP Norber** (4) leads up beneath Robin Proctors Scar. Cross a stile and follow the wall on the right, veering left to climb diagonally just before the wall drops away. At a crossing of ways marked by a finger post, turn left, **FP Norber**, to climb through a rocky nick onto the erratics field (5).

The large gritstone erratics were carried up onto the limestone beds by a glacier which pushed over Moughton during the Ice Age 20,000 years ago, gouging the boulders as it crept down Crummackdale. When the ice sheet finally retreated around 16,500 years ago, the boulders were deposited and left on precarious limestone pedestals.

Eventually drop back down to the wall at a stile just to the left of the lip of a cove formed by Norber Sike. Pass with care onto a narrow path above a cliff along **Nappa Scars** (6).

Here the Great Scar limestone sits upon a layer of coarse conglomerate – a fused mix of pebbles, sand and silt. The path widens and leads down to Crummack Lane (*a short cut, right, on the lane to Austwick cuts 2¼ miles*).

Cross the lane at a stile (7), turning left to cross two fields, over the Sowerthwaite Farm access road and up on a broad green path which climbs towards a nick in the shallow gritstone embankment ahead.

The deeply inclined beds of sandstone (greywacke) plunge into the earth, levelling at a hidden trough (syncline) and rising again further on. These are the ancient Silurian sandstone basement rocks, laid down horizontally, then subsequently squeezed and folded by powerful tectonic movements of the earth's crust, 400 million years ago.

Cross a stile into **Wash Dub Field** – a place where sheep were washed by the little clapper bridge for a popular resting spot (8). Leave the beckside through a wall gap and turn right along the enclosed track heading for **Wharfe**. Turn right through the tiny hamlet and along a walled way to the road, then up along the access road to Wood End Farm for **Feizor**, bearing right by the farm. There's an option to explore Oxenber Woods, otherwise continue to a junction of ways, turning right along the Pennine Bridleway for **Austwick** (9). Cross Austwick Beck at a clapper bridge, and on up to the road. A left takes you through the village, bearing right at the junction.

Cross a stile on the right by a gate, signed **FP Clapham** (10) and bear left diagonally across the field to a wall stile. Continue now along a clear track that follows the contour straight on just north of west, crossing a number of fields to pass through a farm and into Clapham.

L1. Settle to Horton-in-Ribblesdale, *via the Ribble Way* (Maps 1 & 5)

8.5 miles *(13.7 km)* Time: 4:00 Ascent: 350m (Moderate)

A gentle riverside walk along the Ribble Way, with the option to climb Pen-y-ghent.

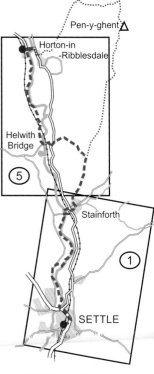

From Settle town centre *(map 1)*, head north along the main street, to cross the River Ribble. Turn right on the *Ribble Way* for *Stackhouse,* climbing above the river and across fields to meet Stainforth Lane. Turn right and follow the quiet lane to Stackhouse. A gate on the right leads down to rejoin the river heading north for *Stainforth*.

Follow the river north, eventually reaching the waterfalls at Stainforth Force. *This is a popular spot and in autumn people gather to watch the salmon as they leap up the falls.* Cross a stile by the old packhorse bridge, turn right and follow the lane up, over the B6479 and into Stainforth.

Pass the car park on the right and at a road junction turn left for *Halton Gill and Arncliffe*, across the next junction into a narrow lane, by the Coach House, signed for *Moor Head Lane*. Cross a ladder stile by a gate, veer left across the field to a stile, then go diagonally right to pass a wall corner.

(Onto map 5) Continue up with the wall on your left, by a ruined barn, following the stream bed when the wall turns away. Pass by a wooded area around How Beck and continue climbing north. Finally climb a wall stile onto a track (Moor Head Lane) that crosses.

If the destination is Pen-y-ghent, head north on a clear path signed *FP Long Lane,* across rough pasture, closing in on the wall on your left. Pen-y-ghent comes into view. Follow the wall, crossing it at one point, until eventually, just beyond a wet patch, you cross a stile to join Long

Stainforth Force

Lane. Follow this NE as it begins to drop, finally meeting the Pennine Way at Churn Mill Hole *(map 7)* and follow it up to the summit.

Otherwise turn left to an enclosed lane and follow it down, turning left again at a lane junction for *Helwith Bridge* to join the route of Walk 5 in reverse.

Go left down the busy B6479, then right on the road to cross *Helwith Bridge*. Take a stile on right for *Foredale* to cross by the pub and over two fields to the quarry road and turn right (*a fieldside path opposite avoids the busy quarry traffic*). Where the road bends left, enter a walled lane on the right under a railway bridge. Where the river bends away to the right, look for wall stile on the left, to cross a small footbridge veering right to a gate. Now follow the wall on the right, on the outside of the walled track, across two stiles and straight over a field towards a farm. Go left past the farm to follow the river all the way to Horton-in-Ribblesdale.

L2. Settle to Horton-in-Ribblesdale, *via Feizor & Crummack Dale* (Maps 2 & 6)

10.4 miles *(16.7 km)* Time: 5:00 Ascent: 530m (Strenuous)

A fine walk to Feizor and Crummack Dale, to climb beside the magnificent limestone terraces at Crummack Dale Head.

From Settle Station *(map 2)* head up through the town to follow the route of Walk 2 by Stackhouse and over Feizor Thwaite to Feizor and its welcome farmhouse café. Now follow the lane north, past the village pump and a row of cottages as the lane swings left to climb, through a gate, between limestone scars. Pass Wharfe Woods *(onto map 6)* on the brow - the coppiced woods are well worth a visit for the abundant wild flowers, particularly in spring and early summer *(look for a stile on the left for access).*

Continue to a stile on the left (*Dales High Way*) and drop across fields to the road, turning left then right into the tiny hamlet. Follow the path around the back by some small cottages to join a walled track heading NW, finally reaching the clapper bridge across Austwick Beck (4).

Now follow the return route for Walk 6 past Crummack Farm and Thieves Moss to Sulber, and down to Horton-in-Ribblesdale via Sulber Nick.

L3. Clapham to Settle, *via Austwick & Feizor* (Maps 3 & 2)

10.0 miles *(16.1 km)* Time: 5:00 Ascent: 500m (Moderate)

A moderately easy walk along the southwest edge of the Dales National Park, with fine long views across the Forest of Bowland throughout.

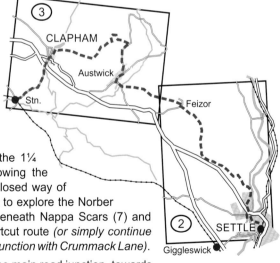

From Clapham Station *(map 3)* walk the 1¼ miles up the road into Clapham, following the route of Walk 3 to join the ancient enclosed way of Thwaite Lane. Take the stile on the left to explore the Norber Erratics (4), joining Crummack Lane beneath Nappa Scars (7) and heading south for Austwick on the shortcut route *(or simply continue along Thwaite Lane and turn right at the junction with Crummack Lane).*

Pass through Austwick and turn left at the main road junction, towards *Settle*, cross Austwick Beck and take the track, left, signed *BW Feizor*. At a left bend cross a stile on a footpath for *Feizor*, go across a field, cross an enclosed path and continue on alongside Oxenber Woods on the left *(onto map 2)* into Feizor.

Now pick up the return route from Walk 2, following the bridleway for *Scar Top* (7), crossing to follow Giggleswick Scar down through Giggleswick and back to Settle.

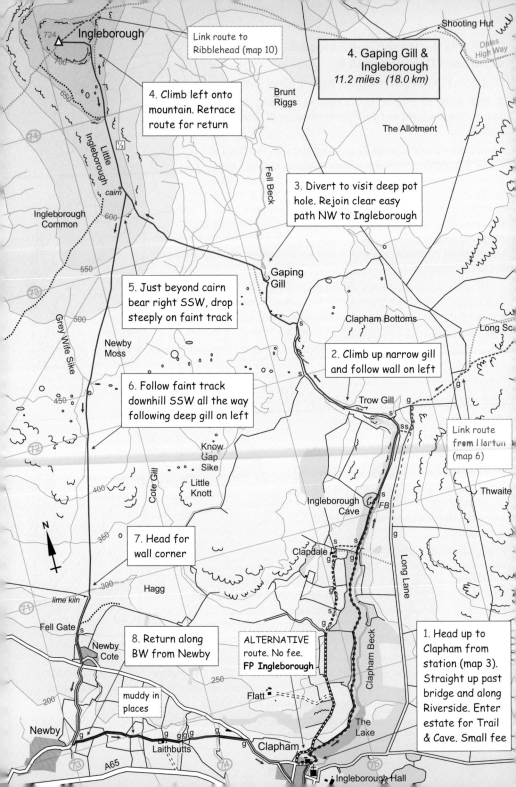

724
Ingleborough
700

Link route to
Ribblehead (map 10)

Shooting Hut

Dales
High Way

**4. Gaping Gill &
Ingleborough**
11.2 miles (18.0 km)

650

4. Climb left onto
mountain. Retrace
route for return

Brunt
Riggs

The Allotment

74

Little
Ingleborough

½

cairn

600

Ingleborough
Common

Fell Beck

3. Divert to visit deep pot
hole. Rejoin clear easy
path NW to Ingleborough

550

Gaping
Gill

5. Just beyond cairn
bear right SSW, drop
steeply on faint track

Clapham Bottoms

Long Sc

73

500

Grey Wife Sike

Newby
Moss

2. Climb up narrow gill
and follow wall on left

Trow Gill

g

Link route
from Horton
(map 6)

450

6. Follow faint track
downhill SSW all the
way following deep gill on left

72

Know
Gap
Sike

Cote Gill

Little
Knott

Ingleborough
Cave

FB

Thwaite

400

Clapdale

7. Head for
wall corner

350

300

lime kiln

Hagg

Long Lane

71

Fell Gate

s

8. Return along
BW from Newby

ALTERNATIVE
route. No fee.
FP Ingleborough

Clapham Beck

1. Head up to
Clapham from
station (map 3).
Straight up past
bridge and along
Riverside. Enter
estate for Trail
& Cave. Small fee

Newby
Cote

muddy in
places

250

Flatt

The
Lake

Newby

200

Laithbutts

A65

73

g

g g g g

g

Clapham

74

Ingleborough Hall

75

4. Gaping Gill & Ingleborough

Clapham 11.2 miles *(18.0 km)* Time: 5:45 Ascent: 720m *Strenuous*

A classic ascent of the area's most iconic mountain, taking in Ingleborough Cave, Trow Gill and Gaping Gill. The ascent route is easy to follow all the way, but the return route crosses rough open pasture and requires clear weather.

Make your way from Clapham Station into the village (see map 3), heading past the bridge along **Riverside** to the entrance of the Ingleborough Estate's **Trail & Cave walk** (1). A small fee is payable. The permissive path passes beside the estate's lake and through the specimen-rich Clapham Woods. A free alternative start can be made just to the east along an enclosed access track for Clapdale Farm signed *FP Ingleborough*.

The track passes **Ingleborough Cave**, first explored and opened up by estate owners, the Farrers, in 1837. *The cave is part of the Gaping Gill system, although the outflow has long since found a lower level, resurging north of the cave entrance at Beck Head. Hour-long tours can be taken in season.*

Beyond, the path curves left into the narrow, steep-sided gorge of **Trow Gill** (2), cut by melt water at the end of the Ice Age. Climb through and alongside the wall on the left, ignoring the first stile (used by potholers) to eventually reach a double ladder stile. A right fork in the track beyond leads to **Gaping Gill** (3), one of the biggest underground caverns in the country into which the waters of Fell Beck plunge. Great care is needed near the rim. *Twice a year members of the public get the chance to descend into the chamber on a cabled chair run by local potholing clubs.*

The clear track now runs NW and soon begins to climb steeply up Little Ingleborough. The path turns north, past a prominent cairn and along the promontory to climb the eastern side of the mountain (4).

The summit is a vast rocky plateau, with excellent panoramic views. The trig point and walkers' shelter are over towards the western end. There are clear remains of prehistoric structures – a wall or embankment which surrounded much of the peak and a series of 20 faint circular structures on the ground, most visible at the southern end. They are believed to be evidence of a 2,000 year-old Iron Age fortified settlement, or possibly a much older Bronze Age religious sanctuary.

Retrace your steps to the cairn at the southern end of Little Ingleborough. Just beyond the cairn bear right, SSW, to pass to the right of rocky piles and descend on a faint track (5). In clear weather the faint path is easy to follow in a straight line, keeping well above the broad deep gill on the left, across Newby Moss (6) *In misty weather, return the same way you came up.*

Drop to a wall corner (7), behind which is a lime kiln, and follow the wall down to the small farming hamlet of **Newby Cote**. Either follow the Old Road left down to Clapham, or cross and take the quiet lane ahead to **Newby**. Just before entering the village, a bridleway on the left leads along the old green Laithbutts Lane to Clapham (8). *A more direct route to the station can be made by passing through Newby, over the busy A65 and down along the quiet road for 1½ miles.*

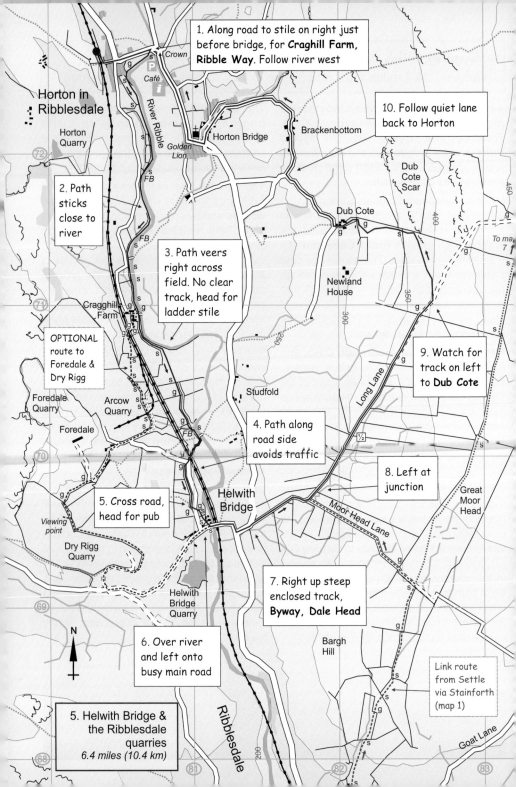

Horton in Ribblesdale

Horton Quarry

Horton Bridge

Golden Lion

FB

Crown

Café

River Ribble

Brackenbottom

Dub Cote Scar

Dub Cote

To ma...
7

Newland House

Cragghill Farm

OPTIONAL route to Foredale & Dry Rigg

Foredale Quarry

Arcow Quarry

Foredale

Studfold

Long Lane

Great Moor Head

Helwith Bridge

Viewing point

Dry Rigg Quarry

Helwith Bridge Quarry

Moor Head Lane

Bargh Hill

N

Ribblesdale

Goat Lane

1. Along road to stile on right just before bridge, for **Craghill Farm, Ribble Way**. Follow river west

2. Path sticks close to river

3. Path veers right across field. No clear track, head for ladder stile

4. Path along road side avoids traffic

5. Cross road, head for pub

6. Over river and left onto busy main road

7. Right up steep enclosed track, **Byway, Dale Head**

8. Left at junction

9. Watch for track on left to **Dub Cote**

10. Follow quiet lane back to Horton

Link route from Settle via Stainforth (map 1)

5. Helwith Bridge & the Ribblesdale quarries
6.4 miles (10.4 km)

5. Helwith Bridge & the Ribblesdale Quarries

Horton-in-R   6.4 miles *(10.4 km)*   Time: 3:00   Ascent: 260m   Easy

A walk of contrasts, between the beautiful wildflower-rich riverside meadows along the Ribble Way and the deep scars of the Ribblesdale quarries.

From Horton-in-Ribblesdale Station walk down to the road eastwards. Just before the bridge take a stile on the right to follow the river back downstream west (1). Follow the riverbank past the water works (2), through riverside meadows, rich with wildflowers in spring and early summer. The road closes in, then pulls away again as you cross a wall to follow the Ribble through a narrow wooded area and on to Cragghill Farm.

*To visit the quarries, at Cragghill Farm turn right to pass through the farm, veering left behind the big barns and along the track to a gate on the right, which leads across a small paddock to a railway crossing. Cross the railway with care, then turn left along a footpath for **Foredale**, veering right to a stile on the far right wall corner. Cross the wall on the right for a short way, crossing back to follow the wall on a raised path, before curving right to drop to a tarmac track which leads up past the entrance to Arcow Quarry.*

*Continue up the road towards the former workers' cottages at **Foredale**, keeping straight on at a steep sharp right bend to Dry Rigg Quarry, following the path around the edge to the left. A viewing platform gives a good vista of the exposed rock strata - a geologist's delight - showing the steeply inclined and folded beds of hard Silurian sandstone and siltstone, now used for road aggregate. Continue around the quarry edge and out along the access road, turning left at the junction to follow the road down to Helwith Bridge, passing the old quarry (now a fishing lake) on the right. Adds 1¼ miles.*

Otherwise continue past Cragghill Farm alongside the river, cross a stile by a gate where the path - signed **Ribble Way** - swings right, away from the track, to cross the field (3). Head for the ladder stile ahead and continue above a wall on the left, eventually crossing it at a stile to join an enclosed track. This track (subject to flooding) swings away from the river and under the railway to reach the road at a gate. Another gate opposite (4) leads to a roadside path, thus avoiding heavy quarry traffic. A gate on the left (5) leads to a footpath across a field for **Helwith Bridge** and the cosy pub by the river.

From the pub car park a stile leads up onto the road and left to cross the bridge (6). Turn left on the main road for a short way to the enclosed track rising on the right signed **Byway Dale Head** (7). Continue left at a junction (8), heading straight up Long Lane towards Pen-y-ghent ahead.

The views across the dale are dramatic, with the three working quarries that scar the landscape all in view: Dry Rigg on the left, with the old water-filled Helwith Bridge Quarry beneath. Arcow (gritstone) in the middle with the old Foredale Quarry above, and the huge Horton Quarry (limestone) on the right. The quarries are an important economic resource for the area. New rail sidings have extended the lives of Arcow and Dry Rigg to 2030. with quarrying at Horton continuing beyond 2040.

Pass through two gates where the gradient begins to ease and look for a gap in the crumbled wall on the left and a faint track for **Dub Cote** (9). *(You can extend the walk here to climb Pen-y-ghent, adding 3 miles, by continuing straight on up to join the Pennine Way at Churn Milk Hole - see map 7).*

The track heads towards a gate before turning left to drop alongside the wall to Dub Cote cottage (a former youth hostel). Pass out onto the road and keep right (10), passing through Brackenbottom to return to Horton-in-Ribblesdale at the bridge by the church.

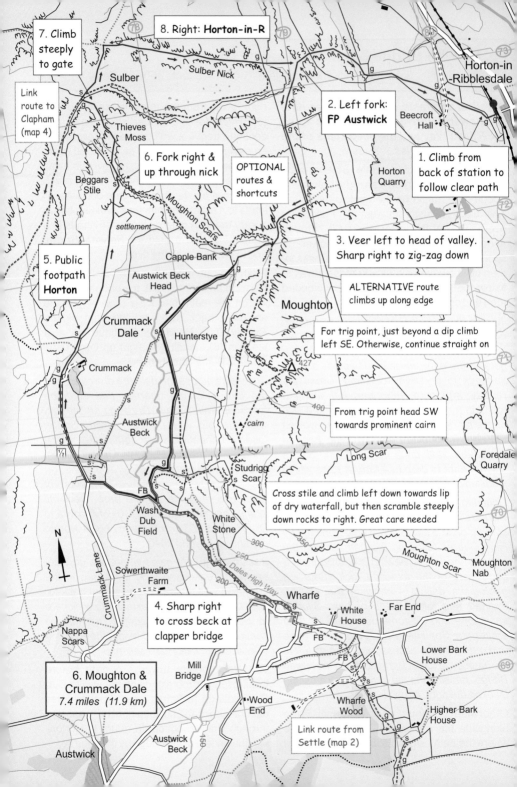

7. Climb steeply to gate

8. Right: Horton-in-R

Sulber Nick

Horton-in-Ribblesdale

Sulber

2. Left fork: FP Austwick

Beecroft Hall

Link route to Clapham (map 4)

1. Climb from back of station to follow clear path

Thieves Moss

6. Fork right & up through nick

OPTIONAL routes & shortcuts

Horton Quarry

Beggars Stile

Moughton Scars

3. Veer left to head of valley. Sharp right to zig-zag down

settlement

5. Public footpath Horton

Capple Bank

Austwick Beck Head

Moughton

ALTERNATIVE route climbs up along edge

For trig point, just beyond a dip climb left SE. Otherwise, continue straight on

Crummack Dale

Hunterstye

△ 427

Crummack

400

From trig point head SW towards prominent cairn

▲ cairn

Austwick Beck

Long Scar

Foredale Quarry

½

Studrigg Scar

FB

Cross stile and climb left down towards lip of dry waterfall, but then scramble steeply down rocks to right. Great care needed

Wash Dub Field

White Stone

300

350

Moughton Scar

Moughton Nab

N

250

Dales High Way

200

Sowerthwaite Farm

Wharfe

White House

Far End

4. Sharp right to cross beck at clapper bridge

FB

Crummack Lane

Lower Bark House

Nappa Scars

Mill Bridge

FB

6. Moughton & Crummack Dale
7.4 miles (11.9 km)

Wharfe Wood

Higher Bark House

Wood End

450

Link route from Settle (map 2)

Austwick

Austwick Beck

An easy walk over classic limestone country into the quiet seclusion and beauty of Crummack Dale, returning across the impressive limestone terraces above Crummack Dale Head.

Climb uphill from the back of Horton-in-Ribblesdale Station following the clear track - the Three Peaks route from Ingleborough (1). Beyond the fourth gate, climb up onto more open fell over limestone outcrops, and as the path levels, beyond a crumbled wall, fork left at a fingerpost signed *FP Austwick* (2).

Make for a gate at a wall corner and follow the wall to cross a ladder stile for **Austwick**. Head straight away perpendicular to the wall, along a line of grouse butts, veering left to the top of a shallow bowl. Drop and swing right, to the edge (3). *Below, lies the rich green valley of Crummack Dale, crisscrossed by ancient packhorse trails. The steep escarpment of Moughton Scars cuts off to the right, with Ingleborough prominent beyond. The juniper-rich limestone pavements across the broad top of Moughton rise gently to the left.*

The main route goes steeply down into the valley, but there are a couple of alternatives – climbing Moughton (left), or an exhilarating shortcut across Moughton Scars to the right.

*For the Moughton alternative, follow the faint track climbing above the edge on the left and continue straight on (optional climb to the trig point), eventually passing the prominent cairn above on the left. The track now drops into bowl, veering right to a ladder stile at a wall above **Studrigg Scar**. Cross the stile then follow the wall steeply down to the left, to reach the lip of a dry waterfall. Don't go over the lip, but scramble down steep rocks to the right hand side, taking care: it's a tricky, rocky scramble. At the foot follow the stream down to a wall, cross the stile, and over fields, leading out onto Hunterstye Lane to rejoin the main route.*

*For the shortcut, turn right and follow the faint track that climbs along the edge above Moughton Scars, passing behind a wall for a while, before rejoining the edge. Cross some deeply-griked limestone paving, before dropping to meet the main route at **Beggars Stile**. The views are magnificent in clear weather, perhaps as impressive as Malham Cove but without the crowds.*

Otherwise drop steeply into the valley, to join a walled track - Hunterstye Lane. Continue down to a junction, turning sharp right here to reach a clapper bridge across Austwick Beck (4) – a popular place for a break.

Follow the walled lane up to the junction with Crummack Lane, turning right here and on to **Crummack Farm**. Pass the farm and follow the wall to the corner and cross a stile by a gate signed **Public Footpath Horton** (5). Go straight on, veering away from the wall on the right, along a clear path, climbing steadily into the limestone amphitheatre of Crummack Dale Head.

There are signs of ancient walling, probably an Iron Age settlement, as you approach the limestone scars.

The path forks - the right hand climbing quickly up a steep nick to **Beggars Stile** (6). Cross the ladder stile and follow the main path through limestone pavement into the slightly wetter area of **Thieves Moss**. The path veers left and climbs steeply up to a gate, onto the green track of Long Lane (7).

Go right through Sulber Gate and on to a crossing of ways (*optionally, follow the fence, right, above Crummack Dale Head, bearing left at the wall to rejoin the main route*) . Turn right at a sign marked **FP Horton in R** (8), to follow the clear path, part of the Three Peaks Route, all the way to Horton-in-Ribblesdale (easier walking can be found on a parallel vehicle track above the edge of Sulber Nick on the right).

L4. Clapham to Ribblehead, *via Ingleborough* (Maps 4 & 10)

9.9 miles *(15.9 km)* Time: 5:15 Ascent: 760m (Strenuous)

A tough but thrilling ridge route across Ingleborough into the heart of Three Peaks country. The finest way to cross this iconic mountain, but strictly in good weather.

From Clapham Station head up the road into Clapham *(see map 3)*, crossing the bridge over the beck. Continue along Riverside to the top of the village *(onto map 4)* and follow the route of Walk 4 to climb Ingleborough via Trow Gill and Gaping Gill, up along the long promontory of Little Ingleborough and onto the summit (4).

From the summit, turn around and head to the north east corner *(onto map 10)* for the descent via Swine Tail, taking great care with the steep drop on the left. Pass through the gate at the foot of the summit (9) to follow the return route for Walk 10 across the ridges of Simon Fell and Park Fell, or the fine alternative route along the western edge. Finish at the oasis that is the Station Inn at Ribblehead .

L6. Horton-in-Ribblesdale to Clapham, *via Long Lane* (Maps 6 & 4)

7.8 miles *(12.6 km)* Time: 3:45 Ascent: 290m (Easy)

An easy, exhilarating walk crossing the head of Crummack Dale and along an ancient drove route to Clapham.

From the station *(map 6)* follow the route for Walk 6. At the left fork for *Austwick* (2), follow the main route left to reach the head of Crummack Dale (3). Here take the stunning shortcut route along the edge of Moughton Scars, with magnificent views down the valley, and through Thieves Moss to join Long Lane by Sulber Gate (7).

Now turn left and follow the easy green track SSW, with long panoramic views of both Pen-y-ghent and Ingleborough. Drop down past Long Scar *(onto map 4)*, through two gates to join the clear lane above Clapham Beck. Either cross a stile on the right to drop steeply down to join the picturesque nature trail from Trow Gill, or continue along Long Lane down into Clapham.

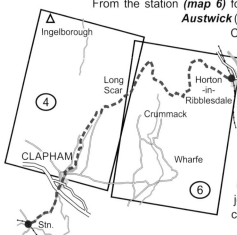

The path to Crummack Dale (above left)
Clapham Beck (above right)
Inside the Hoffmann Kiln (right)
Crossing Moughton Scars (below)

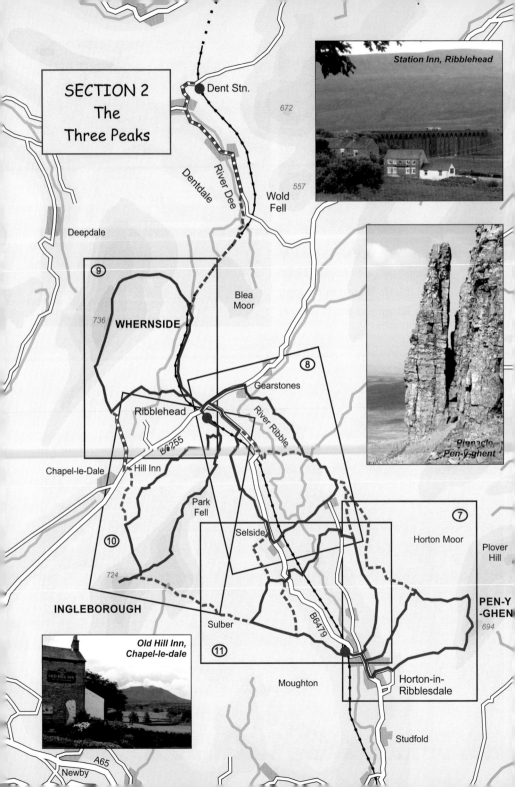

SECTION 2
The
Three Peaks

Station Inn, Ribblehead

672

557

Dent Stn.

Dentdale

River Dee

Wold
Fell

Deepdale

Blea
Moor

⑨

736

WHERNSIDE

*Pinnacle,
Pen-y-ghent*

⑧

Gearstones

Ribblehead

River Ribble

B6255

Chapel-le-Dale

Hill Inn

Park
Fell

Selside

⑩

724

Horton Moor

Plover
Hill

⑦

INGLEBOROUGH

Sulber

B6479

**PEN-Y
-GHENT**

694

⑪

Moughton

Horton-in-
Ribblesdale

*Old Hill Inn,
Chapel-le-dale*

OLD HILL INN

Studfold

A65

Newby

SECTION TWO: The Three Peaks

The landscape of Upper Ribblesdale is dominated by the three mountains of Pen-y-ghent, Ingleborough and Whernside. It was once thought that Ingleborough was the highest peak in England, such is its towering presence, especially as seen from the south west. The peaks attract thousands of visitors each year, many intent on tackling the gruelling Three Peaks Challenge.

The body of the peaks is made up of the banded rocks called Yoredales: repeated layers of limestone, sandstone and shale. The shales erode easily, forming an impervious clay layer which is wet underfoot. The thinner limestone and sandstone beds are much more resistant, forming prominent stepped ledges on the upper flanks of the mountains. The summits are capped with millstone grit.

The peaks themselves sit on top of the Great Scar Limestone, which shows as bright terraces lining the valley sides of Chapel-le-dale and Ribblesdale, before dipping away to the north under layers of glacial till, gently sculpted into rounded drumlins, at Ribblehead.

Today the rough pastures around the peaks serve only for grazing sheep and cattle, but once these hillsides were covered by deciduous woodland. Evidence of this can be seen deep in the limestone grykes, where woodland species such as wood anemone, bluebell, dog's mercury and hartstongue flourish. The trees were cleared by early settlers, but areas of limestone pavement which have been fenced off from grazing soon begin to regenerate natural tree and ground cover. An example can be seen at Sleights, below Ingleborough to the north.

Archaeological evidence of human occupation abounds, especially around Ingleborough, from the earliest Neolithic settlers through to the Viking age and the later medieval monastic lodges. Most fascinating are the enigmatic prehistoric structures on the top of the mountain itself – the subject of ongoing controversy as to what exactly they represent; Iron Age hillfort or Bronze Age religious sanctuary.

The Three Peaks area is crossed by a network of ancient packhorse trails and drove roads that provide excellent walking routes and help explain the scatter of small settlements, some now derelict, which occupy this otherwise bleak landscape.

The gritty little village of Horton-in-Ribblesdale is the only significant settlement here, stretching along the road from the main housing cluster around the railway station to another huddle over half a mile away around St Oswald's Church. This church, which has a curious lean, is the best preserved Norman church in the Dales.

Both ends of the village are served by pubs: the Crown by the bridge at the northern end and the Golden Lion Hotel to the south. Between the two there's a campsite and the Pen-y-ghent café, with its famous factory clocking-in machine.

Quarrying has left deep, ugly scars on the landscape here and the roar of quarry traffic still disturbs the village. Helwith Bridge to the south, with its cosy little pub, is another quarrying settlement although the former Helwith Bridge Quarry is now a fishing lake.

The railway station at Ribblehead (with visitor centre and tea room) is an absolute boon to walkers, but appears to serve no other obvious purpose, there being little habitation save for a few railway cottages nearby and the welcome respite offered by the Station Inn. Yet there was once a bustling settlement of up to two thousand people here – home to the navvies who built the magnificent viaduct. Now there is little to see, unless you know where to look - FoSCL run free tours of the old shanty town site through the summer.

The tiny St Leonard's Church at Chapel-le-Dale has a fitting memorial to those who died whilst building the railway. The hamlet is served by the nearby Old Hill Inn.

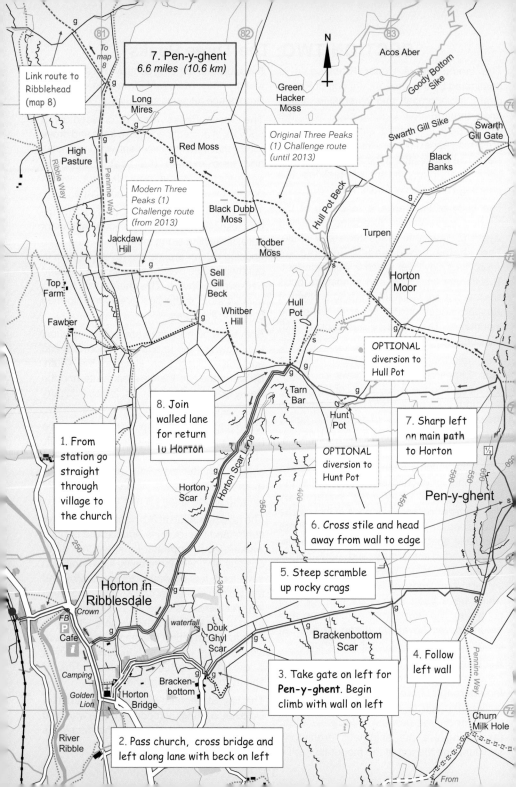

7. Pen-y-ghent
6.6 miles (10.6 km)

N

81
82
83

Acos Aber

Goody Bottom Sike

Link route to Ribblehead (map 8)

To map 8

Long Mires

Green Hacker Moss

Swarth Gill Sike

Swarth Gill Gate

High Pasture

Ribble Way

Pennine Way

Red Moss

Original Three Peaks (1) Challenge route (until 2013)

Black Banks

Hull Pot Beck

Turpen

Modern Three Peaks (1) Challenge route (from 2013)

Black Dubb Moss

Jackdaw Hill

Top Farm

Fawber

Sell Gill Beck

Whitber Hill

Todber Moss

Hull Pot

Horton Moor

g

OPTIONAL diversion to Hull Pot

8. Join walled lane for return to Horton

Horton Scar Lane

Tarn Bar

Hunt Pot

7. Sharp left on main path to Horton

½

1. From station go straight through village to the church

Horton Scar

OPTIONAL diversion to Hunt Pot

Pen-y-ghent

6. Cross stile and head away from wall to edge

5. Steep scramble up rocky crags

Horton in Ribblesdale

Crown

FB

P

Cafe

i

waterfall

Douk Ghyl Scar

Brackenbottom Scar

4. Follow left wall

Churn Milk Hole

Camping

Golden Lion

Horton Bridge

Bracken-bottom

3. Take gate on left for **Pen-y-ghent**. Begin climb with wall on left

Pennine Way

River Ribble

2. Pass church, cross bridge and left along lane with beck on left

From

7. Pen-y-ghent

Horton-in-R   6.6 miles *(10.6 km)*   Time: 3:30   Ascent: 520m   *Strenuous*

A moderately strenuous but short climb to the summit of Pen-y-ghent, the humble mountain that dominates Ribblesdale.

From the station head E down the road, with Pen-y-ghent dominating the view ahead (1). *The distinctive southern profile is marked by two huge ledges, formed by beds of hard limestone at the bottom and gritstone at the top, with the long whaleback running north to Plover Hill.* Cross the bridge by the Crown Inn and turn right to pass through the long village.

At the far end (2) pass St Oswald's Church, cross Horton Bridge and turn left onto the lane. Go on with the beck on the left (3) as the lane climbs, bending right to Brackenbottom. Just before the first barn, take a gate on the left, then a second signed for *Pen-y-ghent*.

It's a steep but straightforward climb, following the wall on the left (4), all the way up to the southern ridge beneath the peak. *The broad terraces of Great Scar Limestone give way at around 400m to rougher grassland covering impervious Yoredale shales.*

Pass through the gate and turn left to begin the climb to the summit (5). The first obstacle – a wall of Main Limestone – blocks the way. The path veers right along the edge and there's a bit of a rocky scramble to get above the limestone lip. The gradient eases a little before the second steep mini-scramble to climb above the gritstone edge. Finally the path rises gently to the summit. *As expected, the views on a clear day are excellent.*

After a suitable rest cross the stile by the trig point and head away from the wall, NW, *Pennine Way, Horton-in-Ribblesdale* (6). The path veers right above the escarpment edge, then descends along the western edge to the foot of the white limestone scars of Pen-y-ghent Side. *In April the western side of the escarpment is adorned with colourful splashes of purple saxifrage, a rare alpine plant seen here at its most southerly reach.*

The well-maintained path now turns sharp left (7), descending steeply. Beyond a gate, a faint track off to the left leads down to the impressive Hunt Pot, which marks the top of the limestone beds. Drop a little further, through a gate to a gate on the left. *A track, right, running north for 300 metres leads to Hull Pot and is well worth the short diversion.*

Turn left through the gate onto the enclosed Horton Scar Lane (8) leading SW down to *Horton-in-Ribblesdale*. At a junction of ways keep right to drop to the road near the café, turning right to return to the station.

The walk can be extended to take in Plover Hill (adding 2.5 miles). From the summit, follow the wall on the right north along the ridge, curving right to the top of Plover Hill. From here drop steeply downhill to join the bridleway crossing from the right at Foxhill Moor. Follow this east to the gateless Swarth Gill Gate and on alongside a wall to Horton Moor. Drop to Hull Pot, then south to rejoin the main route at Horton Scar Lane.

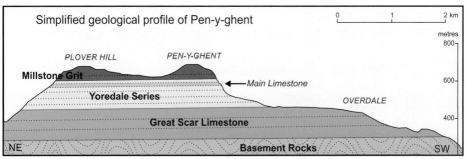

Simplified geological profile of Pen-y-ghent

0   1   2 km

metres

PLOVER HILL   PEN-Y-GHENT

Millstone Grit

Yoredale Series

Main Limestone

OVERDALE

Great Scar Limestone

Basement Rocks

NE   SW

800
600
400

33

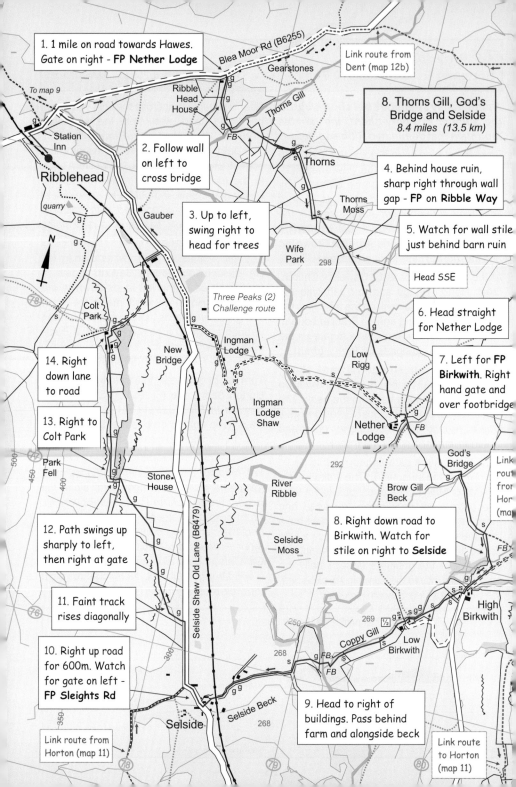

1. 1 mile on road towards Hawes. Gate on right - **FP Nether Lodge**

Blea Moor Rd (B6255)

Gearstones

Link route from Dent (map 12b)

To map 9

Ribble Head House

Thorns Gill

8. Thorns Gill, God's Bridge and Selside
8.4 miles (13.5 km)

FB

Station Inn

Ribblehead

2. Follow wall on left to cross bridge

Thorns

4. Behind house ruin, sharp right through wall gap - **FP on Ribble Way**

quarry

Gauber

3. Up to left, swing right to head for trees

Thorns Moss

5. Watch for wall stile just behind barn ruin

Wife Park   298

Head SSE

N

Three Peaks (2) Challenge route

6. Head straight for Nether Lodge

Colt Park

New Bridge

Ingman Lodge

Low Rigg

7. Left for **FP Birkwith**. Right hand gate and over footbridge

14. Right down lane to road

Ingman Lodge Shaw

Nether Lodge   FB

13. Right to Colt Park

God's Bridge

Link rou from Hor (ma

Park Fell

Stone House

River Ribble

292

Brow Gill Beck

12. Path swings up sharply to left, then right at gate

Selside Moss

8. Right down road to Birkwith. Watch for stile on right to **Selside**

FB

11. Faint track rises diagonally

High Birkwith

Selside Shaw Old Lane (B6479)

250

269   ½

Coppy Gill

Low Birkwith

10. Right up road for 600m. Watch for gate on left - **FP Sleights Rd**

268

FB

FB

9. Head to right of buildings. Pass behind farm and alongside beck

Selside

Selside Beck

268

Link route from Horton (map 11)

Link route to Horton (map 11)

8. Thorns Gill, God's Bridge and Selside

Ribblehead   8.4 miles *(13.5 km)*   Time: 4:00   Ascent: 310m   *Moderate*

A historic round of Upper Ribblesdale, along ancient trails through a landscape of deserted hamlets, former monastic lodges and long forgotten travellers' inns.

From the station walk NE along Blea Moor Rd (B6255) towards Hawes for just under a mile (1), heading towards Gearstones - *a former travellers' inn and market site since medieval times; the last cattle fair took place here in 1872 and the inn finally closed in 1911.* Just past the first building (Ribble Head House) go through a gate signed **FP Nether Lodge**. *You are now on the route of an old packhorse trail which came from Dent and continued south to High Birkwith and on to Horton.* Drop down the field alongside the wall on the left (2), to a beautiful original packhorse bridge over the deep cut of Thorns Gill (*a great place to stop*).

Move up to the left (3), swinging right to pass a wall corner and head for the large house ruin amongst the trees. *This is the deserted old farming hamlet of Thorns, through which passed packhorse men and cattle drovers. The last inhabitant was recorded in 1881.*

Pass to the left of the house, into a walled street. Turn right through a wall gap at the corner (4) and continue straight up over the hill with a wall on the left. *You are crossing one of the finest areas of drumlins in the country - small rounded half-egg-shaped hills of glacial till moulded by the slow passage of ice sheets 20,000 years ago. The going is characteristically wet underfoot.*

Look for a wall stile on the left just beyond a barn ruin (5) and follow the faint track down and up to a stile by a gate at a wall corner. Head up over the hill SSE, dropping and rising, to reach a gate on the hill brow. Head for Nether Lodge (6). *Like Thorns and Colt Park, Nether Lodge began in the 13th century as a monastic lodge for Furness Abbey.*

At Nether Lodge turn left along the farm track signed **FP Birkwith** (7) and through the right

of two gates. Cross the footbridge and follow the clear track up to God's Bridge – *a natural bridge formed by fast moving water cutting under a limestone bed.*

Continue on to cross a stile by a gate, turn right and at the road turn right again to drop to High Birkwith (8). *High Birkwith was once an important monastic grange administering the local holdings of Jervaulx Abbey. In the 18th century it became a coaching inn for traffic coming up from Clapham, passing through Selside and on to Wharfedale.*

Pass through a gate and almost immediately cross a stile on the right for **Selside** (9). Cross diagonally left over two more stiles, through some trees, then drop down following the wall on the right to another stile. Continue down to the beckside heading for the right of the farm at Low Birkwith. Pass through the back of the farm to rejoin the beck on your right.

Go on to cross two footbridges and follow the treeline on your left as it curves round to a walled track. Follow the track, forking right for **Selside**, and under the railway to the hamlet.

Turn right on the main road for 600m (10) to a gate on the left signed **FP Sleights Rd**. A broad green track rises diagonally right (11), up the field through three gates to reach the edge of a rocky terrace by a wooded area. *Looking down to your right, beyond the road, is an excellent view of the drumlin field.*

A path cuts up through the rocky outcrop to the left, towards a gate (12). Just before that gate, turn right along a short enclosed track and right to follow the wall on the left all the way to Colt Park (13). *As the name suggests, it was probably used for monastic horse breeding.* Past Colt Park farmhouse follow the access lane down to the road (14), turn left and go to the T-junction, then left up to the Station Inn *(alternatively past Colt Park, go left through a gate, on to a stile and join the quarry route to Ribblehead - see Walk 10).*

35

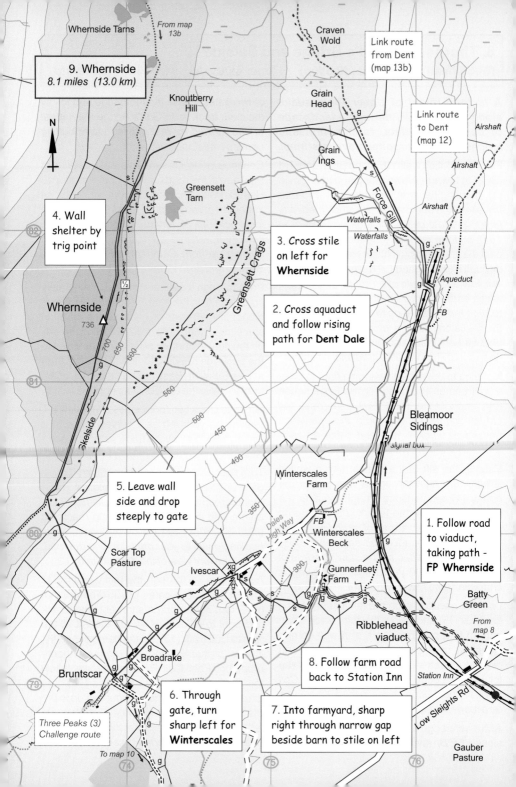

Whernside Tarns

From map 13b

Craven Wold

Link route from Dent (map 13b)

9. Whernside
8.1 miles (13.0 km)

Knoutberry Hill

Grain Head

g

Link route to Dent (map 12)

Airshaft

Grain Ings

Airshaft

N

Greensett Tarn

Airshaft

4. Wall shelter by trig point

s

Waterfalls

82

Force Gill

3. Cross stile on left for Whernside

Greensett Crags

Waterfalls

g

Aqueduct

2. Cross aquaduct and follow rising path for Dent Dale

g

FB

Whernside

736

½

700
650
600

81

Skelside

550

g

Bleamoor Sidings

Signal Box

500

450

5. Leave wall side and drop steeply to gate

400

Winterscales Farm

80

g

350

Dales High Way

FB

1. Follow road to viaduct, taking path - FP Whernside

Scar Top Pasture

Ivescar

xg

Winterscales Beck

Gunnerfleet Farm

300

g

s

g

s

g

s

s

s

g

g

s

Batty Green

From map 8

g

g

g

Ribblehead viaduct

8. Follow farm road back to Station Inn

Broadrake

g

Station Inn

Bruntscar

g

g

79

g

6. Through gate, turn sharp left for Winterscales

7. Into farmyard, sharp right through narrow gap beside barn to stile on left

Low Sleights Rd

Three Peaks (3) Challenge route

g

Gauber Pasture

To map 10

74

75

76

9. Whernside

A moderately strenuous ascent of Yorkshire's highest mountain, following the Three Peaks Challenge route.

Head down the access lane from the station and turn right to pass the Station Inn, then left to follow the road towards the viaduct (1).

The building of the Settle-Carlisle railway between 1869 and 1876 was the last of the great Victorian construction projects. 6,000 people worked on the line at its peak, staying in shanty towns with colourful names such as Belgravia, Sebastopol and Jericho. The largest, at Batty Green (around the road junction down from the Station Inn), was home to as many as 2,000 people. Just east of the viaduct remnants of the brickworks, engine shed, quarries, tramlines and even hut platforms can still be seen.

Before the road turns under the viaduct, take the track – **FP Whernside** – that continues ahead on the right side of the viaduct and climbs up beside the railway. Pass the lonely outpost of Blea Moor signalbox and continue north between beck and rail. *This is the route of an important old packhorse trail from Ingleton to Dent, called the Craven Way. It comes up via Chapel-le-dale to Ellerbeck and then along the eastern foot of Whernside, through Bruntscar, Ivescar and Winterscales.*

The track north from Blea Moor signal box crosses small streams at a couple of spots, before swinging in to cross the railway line by an aqueduct that carries the waters of Force Gill Beck across the line. Continue up the rising path signed **Dent Dale** (2) as it pulls away from the railway to climb steeply alongside a fence, passing the waterfalls of Force Gill. *From this point you can clearly see the row of ventilation shafts that mark the line of the railway as it heads northeast through Blea Moor Tunnel.*

A stile in the fence on the left (3) marks the departure point from this path. Cross and

continue the long climb to **Whernside**. The path closes in to a fence, which then becomes a wall, as it climbs above a steep drop to the left, with Greensett Tarn visible below. The summit is reached at a gap in the wall, with shelters (4). The trig point is on the other side. *On a clear day the views are magnificent, with Morecambe Bay visible to the west, and the Lakeland peaks showing beyond the rounded tops of the Howgill Fells.*

From the summit, continue south with the wall on your right, to begin the long descent. Eventually the path takes a left turn away from the wall (5) and drops straight down steeply, through two gates, to a gate at Bruntscar. *Nearby Bruntscar Hall dates from the mid 17th century and is also the site of Bruntscar Cave. It was a former Cistercian monastic lodge of Jervaulx Abbey.*

Ignore the main track that turns right. Instead, just beyond a barn on the left, take a gate signed **Winterscales** (6).

Follow the clear track all the way to the farm at Ivescar. Pass through a couple of gates into the farmyard. Follow the path sharply to the right (7), passing through a narrow gap beside a barn on your left, through a gate. Immediately there's a stile on your left. Cross this, over the field diagonally to a stile in the left corner ahead.

Continue along this faint track to eventually join another farm road. Turn left, then right through a couple of gates at Gunnerfleet Farm. Continue along the road (8), under the viaduct and back to the Station Inn.

*The walk can be extended from the summit by following the ridge all the way down, past Combe Scar and West Fell, until it begins to level out at North Green. Here drop left and turn, heading NE to follow a clear path, above Twistleton Scars to Ellerbeck. Pass through the farm for **Deepdale** and on to rejoin the main route at Bruntscar. Adds 4 miles.*

L7. Horton-in-R to Ribblehead, *via Pen-y-ghent & Selside*   (Maps 7 & 8)

12.1 miles *(19.4 km)* Time: 6:10 Ascent: 675m (Strenuous)

A tough but exhilarating day's walk climbing Pen-y-ghent and crossing the limestone terraces of Upper Ribblesdale.

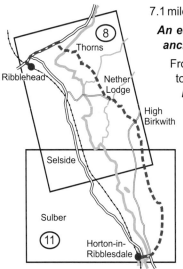

Follow the route of Walk 7 from the station *(map 7)* to climb Pen-y-ghent. Follow the path down from the summit to the gate at the top of Horton Scar Lane (8), but don't go through. Instead continue west following the **Yorkshire Three Peaks (Y3P)** route for **High Birkwith via Whitber Hill**. Continue west, climbing with the wall on your left to the brow of Whitber Hill.

Just over the brow of the hill at a wall corner, keep to the clear track sharp left heading west. Drop gently to pass through a gate in the wall ahead, then veer right to cross the beck and continue up along the clear track, climbing over a wet hillside. The track curves left and descends to a gate on the right, then down to join the **Pennine Way** and **Y3P** for **High Birkwith** heading north.

Leave the Pennine Way at a gate, left, and continue to follow the **Y3P** route NW *(onto map 8)*. Cross a wall stile by a gate and turn left onto the access road above High Birkwith, to join the route of Walk 8 for Ribblehead via Selside.

L8. Ribblehead to Horton-in-Ribblesdale, *via the Ribble Way*   (Maps 8 & 11)

7.1 miles *(11.5 km)*   Time: 3:30 Ascent: 260m (Easy)

An easy walk along part of the Ribble Way, following an ancient packhorse route.

From Ribblehead Station *(map 8)* follow the route of walk 8, to join the Ribble Way at Thorns. Continue on past *Nether Lodge* to join the access road to *High Birkwith* (8).

Here turn left up the access road and veer sharp right at a fork to cross a wall stile by a gate. Follow the track south a little way above a wooded gorge, but here bear right onto a broad terrace beneath limestone scars on the left. Follow the track south, dropping to cross a stile and a shallow gorge ahead, bearing right to pick up the broad, lush green terrace again, continuing south. Cross a couple of stiles to join the route *(onto map 11)* in reverse from Far Moor Bridge to Horton, bearing left past a barn ruin (2), over a stile to join the Pennine Way at Sell Gill Holes. Turn right to follow this down into Horton.

L9. Ribblehead to Dent, *via Blea Moor* (Maps 9 & 12)

6.7 miles *(10.7 km)* Time: 3:30 Ascent: 410m (Moderate)

Follow the hidden line of the Settle-Carlisle railway over Blea Moor with long views of Chapel-le-dale and Dentdale.

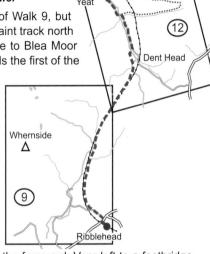

From Ribblehead Station *(map 9)* follow the route of Walk 9, but instead of crossing the aqueduct (2), continue on a faint track north along the right side of the railway, past the entrance to Blea Moor Tunnel and over the beck heading straight up towards the first of the railway ventilation shafts. The path now becomes clear, continuing NE, rising between two more double spoil heaps ahead. Cross a stile and continue in a straight line *(onto map 12)*. Another airshaft appears ahead as you begin to drop to the forest. Continue through the trees and cross the forest track, straight ahead, descending steeply.

Cross a stile and follow the wall on your right to drop over the spoil heap. The railway emerges from the tunnel on your right. Swing left, through a wall gap with the beck on your right, passing a series of mini waterfalls. Cross a footbridge and go on with the beck on the left to Dent Head Farm. A gate leads through the farmyard. Veer left to a footbridge, through a gate and follow the track across the open field north. The track closes to a fence on the right, over a footbridge to the road at Bridge End. Now follow the road left (9), passing Cow Dub and the Sportsman's Inn (give yourself 45 minutes to the station from the pub if taking a break). Continue down to Lea Yeat and up the steep climb to Dent Station.

(An optional climb up Arten Gill from Stone House, along the old drove road on the western flank of Great Knoutberry, returning to the station on the Coal Rd, adds 3 miles and 1½ hours.)

Dent Head Viaduct from Blea Moor

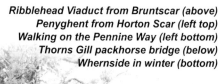

Ribblehead Viaduct from Bruntscar (above)
Penyghent from Horton Scar (left top)
Walking on the Pennine Way (left bottom)
Thorns Gill packhorse bridge (below)
Whernside in winter (bottom)

The Three Peaks Challenge Route

The Yorkshire Three Peaks Challenge - climbing Whernside, Ingleborough and Pen-y-ghent and returning to the starting point in a continuous circuit – is a tough undertaking. Covering a distance of around 24 miles, with a total ascent of over 1,600 metres, completing the route in under 12 hours is considered a notable achievement.

There is no official route or starting point to the Three Peaks Challenge, so you won't find it marked on OS maps, though the most popular route (*shown over page*) is now well established. Many choose to start at Horton-in-Ribblesdale, but Ribblehead, with its early morning train service makes a better starting point. Whernside is climbed first, then ingleborough, leading down to Horton-in-Ribblesdale. Pen-y-ghent follows, then there's a seven-mile trek over Horton Moor to finish back at Ribblehead.

The modern route follows mostly well maintained and signed paths, much of them slab-paved around the summits themselves, to avoid erosion. Since 2013 the once notorious section over the boggy quagmire of Black Moss Dubb has been replaced with a well engineered track over Whitber Hill.

In recent years the Challenge has become increasingly popular, particularly as a fund-raiser for charities. It is now not unusual on summer weekends or bank holidays to see over 1,000 people a day set out on the route. This has caused real problems for many residents of Horton.

If you are thinking of tackling the Three Peaks Challenge, you are better to avoid weekends and bank holidays. Avoid an early morning start in Horton - consider a different starting point like Ribblehead.

Since 1954 the annual spring Three Peaks Fell Race (which follows a slightly different course) has become one of the top international fell races, with up to a thousand runners entering, the best completing the circuit in well under three hours.

Though a worthy endurance challenge, this 24-mile slog is not the best way to get to know the Three Peaks themselves. It is much better to spend a few days in the area, stopping at an inn or B&B and using the train to tackle the peaks individually, as the walks in this book allow. Take time to explore and appreciate these very different, modest but beautiful mountains.

This is also the best way to prepare for the endurance walk - taking on the Three Peaks Challenge should certainly not be your first introduction to the area. Perhaps having explored the mountains at a more leisurely pace, the need to put yourself through the gruelling trial will seem less important.

in 2018 the town of Ingleton was promoted as an alternative start and finish point. This route is even tougher, at a little under 30 miles and with additional ascent.

If you do take on the Challenge, consider joining the *Friends of the Three Peaks*, which helps to protect and enhance the inspirational landscape of the Three Peaks area.

Fell runners tackle the Three Peaks (photo: Julia Pearson)

Deepdale

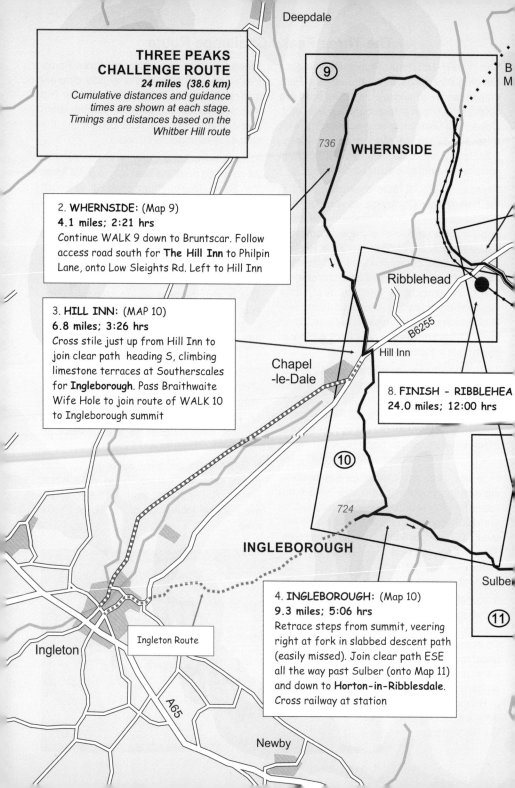

**THREE PEAKS
CHALLENGE ROUTE**
*24 miles (38.6 km)
Cumulative distances and guidance
times are shown at each stage.
Timings and distances based on the
Whitber Hill route*

⑨

B
M

736   **WHERNSIDE**

**2. WHERNSIDE: (Map 9)
4.1 miles; 2:21 hrs**
Continue WALK 9 down to Bruntscar. Follow
access road south for **The Hill Inn** to Philpin
Lane, onto Low Sleights Rd. Left to Hill Inn

Ribblehead

**3. HILL INN: (MAP 10)
6.8 miles; 3:26 hrs**
Cross stile just up from Hill Inn to
join clear path heading S, climbing
limestone terraces at Southerscales
for **Ingleborough**. Pass Braithwaite
Wife Hole to join route of WALK 10
to Ingleborough summit

Chapel
-le-Dale

B6255

Hill Inn

8. FINISH - RIBBLEHEA
24.0 miles; 12:00 hrs

⑩

724

INGLEBOROUGH

Sulbe

⑪

Ingleton Route

Ingleton

**4. INGLEBOROUGH: (Map 10)
9.3 miles; 5:06 hrs**
Retrace steps from summit, veering
right at fork in slabbed descent path
(easily missed). Join clear path ESE
all the way past Sulber (onto Map 11)
and down to **Horton-in-Ribblesdale**.
Cross railway at station

A65

Newby

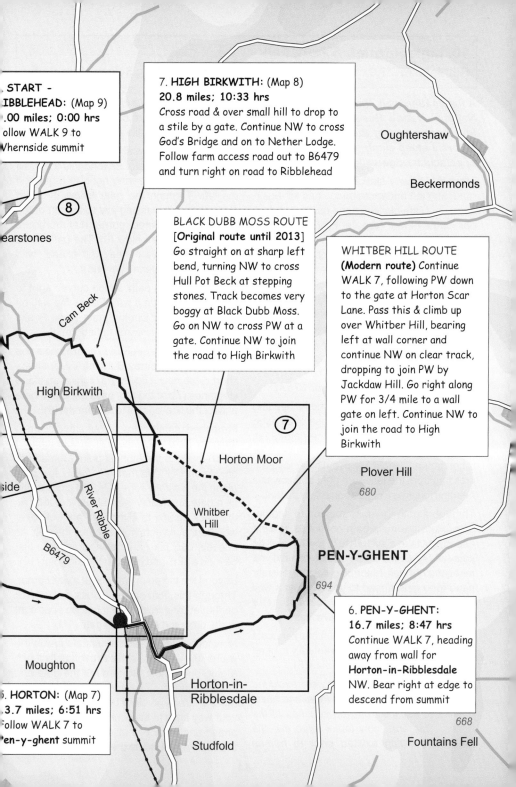

START -
RIBBLEHEAD: (Map 9)
0.00 miles; 0:00 hrs
Follow WALK 9 to
Whernside summit

7. HIGH BIRKWITH: (Map 8)
20.8 miles; 10:33 hrs
Cross road & over small hill to drop to
a stile by a gate. Continue NW to cross
God's Bridge and on to Nether Lodge.
Follow farm access road out to B6479
and turn right on road to Ribblehead

Oughtershaw

Beckermonds

⑧

earstones

BLACK DUBB MOSS ROUTE
[**Original route until 2013**]
Go straight on at sharp left
bend, turning NW to cross
Hull Pot Beck at stepping
stones. Track becomes very
boggy at Black Dubb Moss.
Go on NW to cross PW at a
gate. Continue NW to join
the road to High Birkwith

WHITBER HILL ROUTE
(**Modern route**) Continue
WALK 7, following PW down
to the gate at Horton Scar
Lane. Pass this & climb up
over Whitber Hill, bearing
left at wall corner and
continue NW on clear track,
dropping to join PW by
Jackdaw Hill. Go right along
PW for 3/4 mile to a wall
gate on left. Continue NW to
join the road to High
Birkwith

Cam Beck

High Birkwith

Horton Moor

⑦

Plover Hill

680

side

River Ribble

Whitber
Hill

B6479

PEN-Y-GHENT

694

6. PEN-Y-GHENT:
16.7 miles; 8:47 hrs
Continue WALK 7, heading
away from wall for
Horton-in-Ribblesdale
NW. Bear right at edge to
descend from summit

Moughton

668

5. HORTON: (Map 7)
13.7 miles; 6:51 hrs
Follow WALK 7 to
Pen-y-ghent summit

Horton-in-
Ribblesdale

Studfold

Fountains Fell

10. Ingleborough & Park Fell

Ribblehead   **8.9 miles** *(14.4 km)*   Time: **4:30**   Ascent: **540m**   *Strenuous*

A fascinating walk through Ingleborough National Nature Reserve and along the limestone scars at the mountain's base, before a steep climb to the summit and a spectacular ridge walk to Park Fell.

From the railway station, head down to the road, turn left under the bridge and left again to go up to the old limestone quarry (1), now part of the nature reserve. Follow the green marker posts (2), bearing left to leave the quarry at its eastern edge. Climb through two gates and continue to follow the marker posts on a faint path which curves right, above the limestone pavement, eventually curving back north. Just 20m further west the remains of a Viking age settlement (SD 765784) can be seen. *Excavated in 1975, the remains of a long house, two workshops and enclosure walls are visible. Anglo-Saxon coins (stycas) found there date the site to around 875 AD.*

Turn back to follow a path south, heading towards Park Fell along the base of a raised plateau on your right (3). As the path fades continue in a straight line, now climbing over rough ground, to join a faint but clear footpath crossing from the left. Turn right to follow this heading towards a copse some way distant.

Through a gate the path goes on to another gate. Here the main path continues straight ahead, but take a left fork to follow the wall on your left (4). Cross a stile and go on until you meet another wall. Ignoring gates on your left, head for a gate ahead to your right at a wall corner, which leads back into the *Ingleborough National Nature Reserve*.

Follow the **Ridge Route** green marker posts straight ahead, curving left eventually to head back up to join the wall on your left (5).

To the right grazing livestock were excluded for many years allowing ash trees and hazel bushes to escape from the confines of the grikes. This area now looks more like the landscape which existed prior to human clearance of the upland woodlands that once covered the Yorkshire Dales. Continue SW to eventually reach a stile and gate on your left.

Continue, with the wall now on your right, to another stile and gate. Beyond this a narrow enclosure leads, veering right, to a gate on the left. Through the gate follow the path straight ahead, passing just to the left of the enclosed, tree-lined gorge that harbours Great Douk cave below (6). The path veers left up to a gate in the wall ahead, with Ingleborough towering beyond it.

Continue on this path, which curves right to cross a stile above a wall. Follow the wall on your right now to join the main Three Peaks path heading left towards Ingleborough.

The path climbs steeply over board walks and flagging to Humphrey Bottom. A very steep, short climb now follows, zigzagging up stone steppings (7). At the top, pass through a gate and for the final ascent to the summit (8).

From the summit, retrace your steps down to the gate. Now follow the wall on your right (9) which leads to the highest point (unmarked) on Simon Fell *(alternatively follow the path along the western edge)*. Drop to cross a stile by a gate and follow the wall on your left . As the track begins to climb up Park Fell, over wet ground, it veers right to leave the wall. As it levels out, take a crossing track left, just beyond a tarn, and head for the trig point (10).

Beyond the trig point is a gate at a wall corner. Through this, immediately cross a stile back on the left and follow the fence on your right north, dropping steeply to a gate (11).

Now follow a track which runs alongside the wall on the left, past a stile to eventually reach a gate on the left. Go through the gate and continue north, following the wall on your right. There is no clear track here, but make your way back to the walkers' gate in the wall ahead and retrace your steps down through the quarry and back to the station.

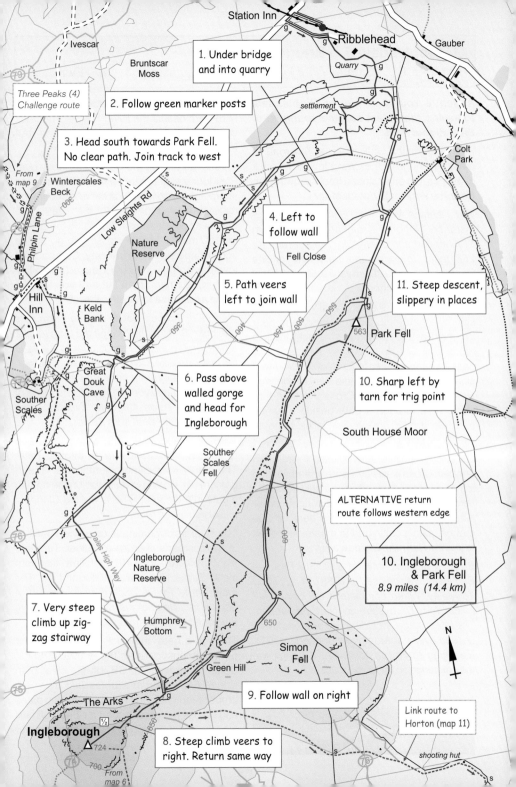

11. Ribblesdale & a Bridge to Far Moor

Horton-in-R   7.3 miles *(11.8 km)*   Time: 3:30   Ascent: 310m   *Easy*

A gentle round of Upper Ribblesdale following the oldest and the youngest of the national trails.

From the station walk down to the road to cross the bridge by the Crown Inn. At the back of the pub join an enclosed track following the **Pennine Way** for **Birkwith Moor** (1).

The Pennine Way was Britain's first long-distance National Trail, created by Tom Stephenson and opened in 1965. It runs for 268 miles following the backbone of the Pennines from the Derbyshire Peak District to the Scottish Borders.

The track climbs steadily, finally reaching a stile by a gate onto Open Access land near Whitber Pasture. Continue on a rocky track to reach Sell Gill Holes. Cross the beck and pass through a gate, forking left to drop to a stile (2), leaving the Pennine Way to continue along the **Ribble Way**. Cross this then turn sharp right through a gate beside a ruined barn. Go straight on, over two stiles, beneath limestone scars on the right.

Go through a gate above Scale Farm, then another. Cross a stile by a gate ahead, forking left on a signed footpath diagonally down the field (3) to a gate at the bottom right corner leading onto a road. Turn right here for 200 metres, past a cattle grid to a gate on the left to join the **Pennine Bridleway** (4).

Britain's newest national trail, the Pennine Bridleway, was devised in 1986 by Lady Mary Towneley. When complete it will cover 347 miles from Derbyshire to Northumberland. The latest stage, including this new bridleway section over Far Moor, was opened in 2011. Reaching to Ravenstonedale, it brings the total distance so far to 200 miles.

Follow the track as it drops down to pass Dale Mire Barn beside the River Ribble. The track curves left, leading to the hidden but impressive Far Moor Bridleway Bridge.

Across the bridge, the clear track leads over Far Moor and under the railway line, swinging sharp right up to a wall corner and continuing up into a walled way to the road. The bridleway now leads out alongside the B6479 for 100 metres before crossing to go up the access lane signed **Bridleway, Clapham** (6) towards Borrins & South House Farm. The lane swings right, then left and you leave it along a track that forks off to the left.

*A shortcut through **South House Farm** cuts one mile. Go straight through the farm to take a gate on the left and cross over to a stile in the wall opposite. Climb up past a wall corner. Continue straight on, beneath the limestone escarpment up to your right, with fine views of Pen-y-ghent across the dale. Eventually join the Three Peaks path from Sulber.*

The main track joins a wall on the right and on to a gate, then swings left to another gate. The track now climbs gently over rough pasture (8), closing in on a wall on the right to a gate in the corner. *This is the old Clapham to Selside green road.*

The clear track continues over open pasture to a crossroads of paths at Sulber. Turn left, signed **Horton-in-R** (9) to follow the path along Sulber Nick towards Horton (10). *The main Three Peaks track is quite eroded. A parallel vehicle track just up to the right above the edge makes for much easier walking.*

Through a gate, the track drops to another path junction, where the shortcut joins. Continue straight on, SE, on the clear path signed *FP Horton in Ribblesdale*. The path drops steeply, curving right through two gates and across the access road for Beecroft Hall (11), before dropping across a short field to the station.

46

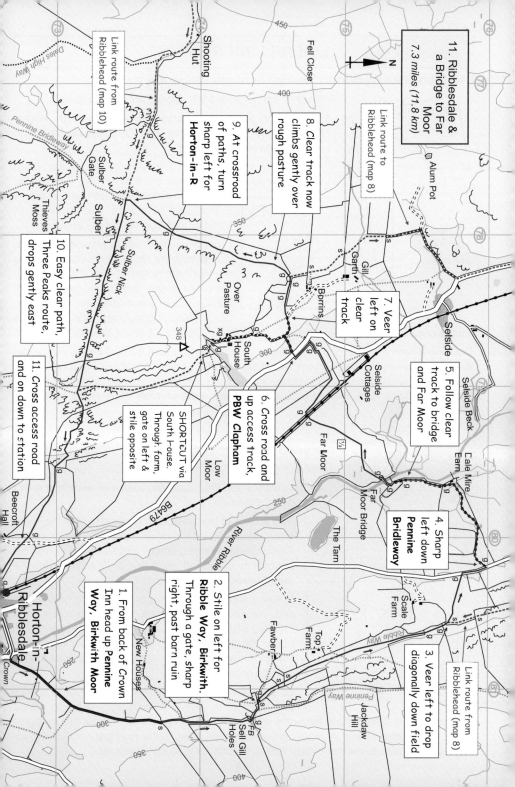

11. Ribblesdale & a Bridge to Far Moor
7.3 miles (11.8 km)

N

Link route to Ribblehead (map 8)

Link route from Ribblehead (map 10)

9. At crossroad of paths, turn sharp left for Horton-in-R

8. Clear track now climbs gently over rough pasture

7. Veer left on clear track

5. Follow clear track to bridge and Far Moor

10. Easy clear path, Three Peaks route, drops gently east

6. Cross road and up access track, PBW Clapham

4. Sharp left down Pennine Bridleway

SHORTCUT via South House. Through farm, gate on left & stile opposite

11. Cross access road and on down to station

1. From back of Crown Inn head up Pennine Way, Birkwith Moor

2. Stile on left for Ribble Way, Birkwith. Through a gate, sharp right, past barn ruin

3. Veer left to drop diagonally down field

Link route from Ribblehead (map 8)

Horton-in-Ribblesdale

L10. Ribblehead to Horton, *via Ingleborough* (Maps 10 & 11)

9.0 miles *(14.4 km)* Time: 4:20 Ascent: 460m (Moderate)

A moderately easy, quick climb up Ingleborough, with a long, steady descent along the Three Peaks route to Horton-in-Ribblesdale.

Follow the route of Walk 10 from Ribblehead Station *(map 10)*, around the quarry to the foot of Park Fell and on through the national nature reserve, before the steep climb to the summit of Ingleborough from Humphrey Bottom.

From the summit, initially retrace your steps, descending the steep, stone stairway along the northern edge of the mountain top. Watch for a right fork in the slabbed path, easily missed. This bears east, dropping to join a broad, stoney track, with long views south along the prominence of Little Ingleborough, with Gaping Gill below, towards Clapham.

Crossing a wall at a stile, the track descends past the southern flank of Simon Fell, again slabbed, to eventually reach an old, ruined shooting hut *(onto map 11)*. Follow a wall on the left to pass through a narrow gap between limestone outcrops to a gate. Continue east to a crossing of paths at Sulber, to pick up the return route of Walk 11 down to *Horton-in-Ribblesdale*.

L11. Horton to Ribblehead, *via Selside* (Maps 11 & 8)

6.3 miles *(10.1 km)* Time: 3:00 Ascent: 250m (Easy)

An easy walk along limestone terraces with excellent views across Ribblesdale.

From the back of Horton Station *(map 11)* follow the Three Peaks Route (Walk 11 in reverse) towards Ingleborough. Climb over limestone outcrops and as the path levels out beyond a crumbled wall, by a fingerpost for *FP Ingleborough*, turn right (unmarked).

Follow a faint track between the wall below on the right and the limestone scars on the left, heading north *(marked SHORTCUT on the map)*. Pass through South House Farm and out along the access road. Bear left at the junction and left again (7) to follow a clear track forking from the access road.

Go through a couple of gates and turn right, on to cross a stile northwards. Cross the field veering left to a stile. Continue to a wall corner and follow the outside of the wall on your left, over a stile by a gate and into an enclosed way. A sharp right ahead leads down to the road just north of Selside *(onto map 8)*. Now follow the route of Walk 8, via Colt Park, on to Ribblehead.

Ingleborough & Whernside from Mallerstang

Dent Station - the highest in England (above)
Yore Bridge (right)
Garsdale from above Dandra Garth (below)

SECTION THREE: Dentdale & Garsdale

The bleak, wild, high country around the heads of Dentdale and Garsdale marks the point of the Yorkshire Dales where, on the wet mossy fell tops, the rivers of the Dales begin their journey seawards, etching deep valleys in all directions.

North is the valley of Mallerstang, where the mighty River Eden begins its life high on Lunds Fell. Just metres away another trickle bears east, growing to become the River Ure as it starts its long meandering course down Wensleydale to the North Sea. The River Lune skirts the Howgill Fells, collecting all the waters from the western dales before finally turning west on its way to Morecambe Bay. The River Ribble rises on Cam Fell and heads south down Ribblesdale, crossing Lancashire to the Irish Sea at Blackpool.

The Great Scar Limestone is mostly deeply buried, showing in the valley bottoms of Dentdale and Garsdale. Here the land is dominated by the Yoredales: the shales giving wet, rough tracts; the thin limestone and sandstone beds producing long stretches of dry, springy turf and lovely stepped cascades of water. The highest peaks are topped by millstone grit.

18,000 years ago, most of the Dales were covered in ice, with only the topmost peaks jutting out like tiny islands. The Dales ice sheet was centred around Baugh Fell, pushing down and carving the river valleys into wide, U-shaped glacial valleys.

The two railway stations that serve this area are isolated. Dent, the highest mainline station in England, lies a full 4¼ miles from the village it serves. Garsdale's nearest towns are Hawes to the east (5¼ miles) and Sedbergh to the west (9½ miles). The nearest pubs, *the Sportsman's* in Cowgill and *the Moorcock* at Garsdale Head, are both a substantial walk from the stations.

At the time of writing, there is a limited daily bus service between Garsdale Station and Hawes, and a very limited service on Saturday from Dent Station, but these are subject to change so need checking. Careful planning and timing are essential here.

Yet this is truly stunning walking country, the wide open fells offering space, solitude and some of the best views you'll find in the Dales.

A network of ancient trade routes crosses this high country, making fine walking routes. The High Way, running above Mallerstang, served drovers coming south from Scotland to Hawes, or climbing the Galloway Gate into Dentdale, or over Wold Fell to Gearstones in Ribblesdale. The Craven Way is another old packhorse trail that climbs from Dentdale over to Chapel-le-dale on the way to Ingleton.

Dentdale is perhaps the most beautiful of the Yorkshire Dales, its lush meadows justly famous for their magnificent summer wildflower displays. The many distinct farmsteads, strung along each side of the dale, reflect their Scandinavian origins. Dent village is a popular tourist destination, with good accommodation, including campsites, shop, cafes, two pubs and a heritage centre.

Garsdale is a quiet valley, with no village as such, just a scattering of houses and farms, some clustered together, but boasting a church and three chapels.

Wensleydale is one of the best known of the Yorkshire Dales, with Hawes – the highest market town in the Dales - at its head.

In 1878 Garsdale Station was known as Hawes Junction, from which passenger trains ran the 40 miles along the Wensleydale railway to link with the east coast main line at Northallerton. The line finally closed in 1992, but in 2000 the Wensleydale Railway Association was formed to secure the track, begin restoring stations and running steam and diesel services for visitors and local passengers. Trains currently run regularly at the eastern end of the dale between Redmire and Leeming Bar, but the Association hope one day to reconnect the line to Garsdale, thus restoring one of the most beautiful railway journeys in the country.

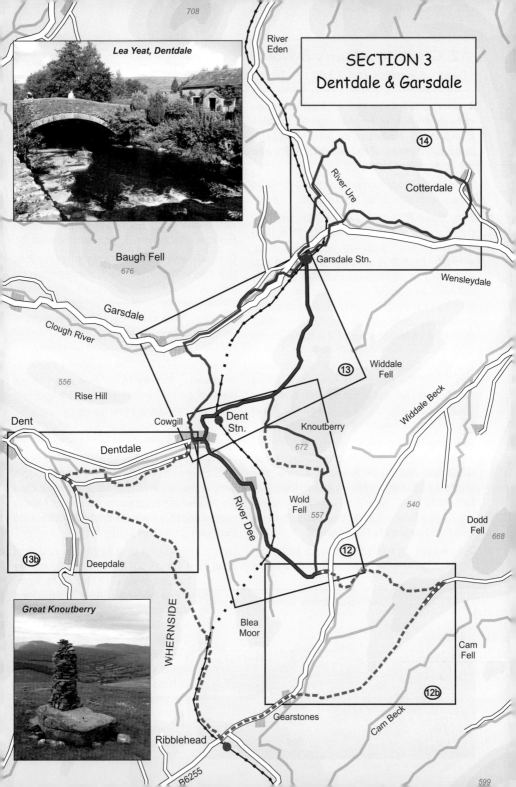

708

River Eden

Lea Yeat, Dentdale

River Ure

Cotterdale

⑭

Baugh Fell
676

Garsdale Stn.

Wensleydale

Garsdale

Clough River

556

Rise Hill

Widdale Fell

⑬

Widdale Beck

Dent

Cowgill

Dentdale

Dent Stn.

Knoutberry
672

⑬b

Deepdale

Wold Fell
557

540

Dodd Fell
668

River Dee

⑫

Great Knoutberry

WHERNSIDE

Blea Moor

Cam Fell

⑫b

Gearstones

Cam Beck

Ribblehead

B6255

599

12. Great Knoutberry & Wold Fell

Dent   8.8 miles *(14.2 km)*   Time: **4:30**   Ascent: **590m**   *Strenuous*

A good start from the highest mainline railway station in England gives a quick climb onto Knoutberry with fantastic panoramic views of the western Dales and the upper Eden Valley.

From Dent Station turn right on the Coal Road (1) and walk steeply up to a junction.

The Coal Road is part of an ancient packhorse and drove trail leading from Dent over to Garsdale and north into Mallerstang, along the High Way to Kirkby Stephen. It was also used to serve the extensive Garsdale collieries on Cowgill Head (hence its name). Thin seams of poor quality coal were mined there for hundreds of years up to the mid 19th century and the coming of the railway. The road to Garsdale beyond the junction is known as Galloway Gate, getting its name partly from the galloways (ponies) used as packhorses for transporting the coal and other goods, and partly as it was the drove road for Scottish cattle from Galloway.

Turn right through a gate along an enclosed track (2), signed **Pennine Bridleway, Arten Gill Moss** and go on to reach a gate *(this branch off Galloway Gate is known locally as the Driving and again was part of the old drove road from Scotland that leads down via Newby Head Gate to Gearstones).*

Take a gate on the left to cross a small pen (3), through another gate and turn to follow the fence on your left uphill. Where the slope begins to ease, pass a line of prominent cairns running off on the right, and go on to the summit. *Here there are extensive panoramic views including: the Three Peaks, and Pendle Hill to the south; Great Coum, Middleton Fell and Rise Hill to the west with the Howgills beyond; Baugh Fell, Wild Boar Fell, Mallerstang Edge and Great Shunner Fell to the north; with Dodd Fell to the east.*

Continue with the wall on your left (4) to drop to a stile and onto the track which comes up from Arten Gill and continues east down Widdale and on to Hawes. Go right and follow the track down to a gate. *(To take a shortcut here go through the gate and down Arten Gill to Stone House Bridge, cutting 2½ miles.)*

Before the gate turn left (5) signed **Pennine Bridleway, Newby Head Road** and follow the wall on the right heading south to climb the western slope of Wold Fell.

As you climb, the broad green track pulls away from the wall to pass through the saddle of a shallow dry valley (6), with good views NE of Widdale. Continue, curving round to a gate to join an enclosed track. Another gate leads down a clear track to the road at Newby Head Gate *(the Pennine Bridleway heads left here - see Link Walk L12).*

Now turn right for a long three-mile stretch of quiet road, joining the route of the **Dales Way** to Lea Yeat (7). The Dent Road drops steeply under Dent Head Viaduct (8) and alongside the young River Dee (9). Cross Stone House Bridge (10), beneath Arten Gill Viaduct *(built of a dark limestone called Dent Marble)*, and continue with the river now on your right, past the Sportsman's Inn and down to Lea Yeat Bridge. Cross the bridge (11) and join the Coal Road as it rises steeply back up to the station.

Looking south from Great Knoutberry Hill

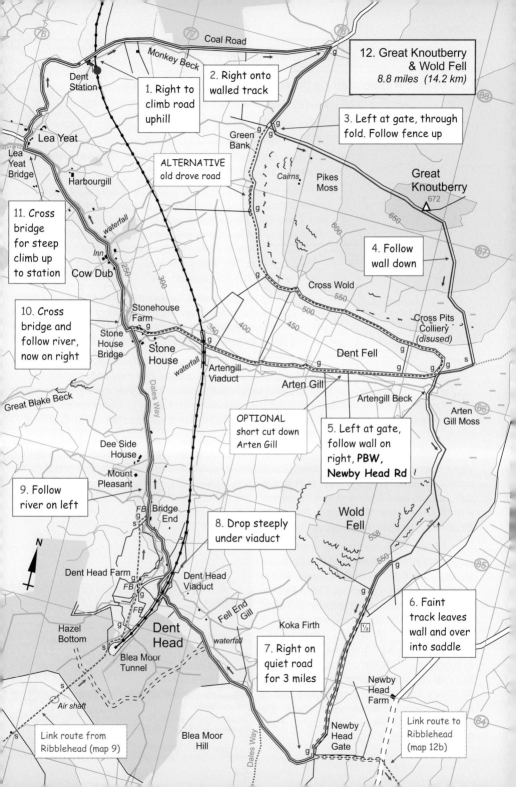

12. Great Knoutberry & Wold Fell
8.8 miles (14.2 km)

1. Right to climb road uphill

2. Right onto walled track

3. Left at gate, through fold. Follow fence up

4. Follow wall down

5. Left at gate, follow wall on right, PBW, Newby Head Rd

6. Faint track leaves wall and over into saddle

7. Right on quiet road for 3 miles

8. Drop steeply under viaduct

9. Follow river on left

10. Cross bridge and follow river, now on right

11. Cross bridge for steep climb up to station

ALTERNATIVE old drove road

OPTIONAL short cut down Arten Gill

Link route from Ribblehead (map 9)

Link route to Ribblehead (map 12b)

Dent Station
Lea Yeat
Lea Yeat Bridge
Harbourgill
Cow Dub
Inn
waterfall
Green Bank
Cairns
Pikes Moss
Great Knoutberry
672
Cross Wold
Cross Pits Colliery (disused)
Dent Fell
Arten Gill
Artengill Beck
Arten Gill Moss
Stonehouse Farm
Stone House Bridge
Stone House
waterfall
Artengill Viaduct
Great Blake Beck
Dales Way
Dee Side House
Mount Pleasant
Bridge End
FB
Dent Head Farm
FB
FB
Hazel Bottom
Dent Head
Blea Moor Tunnel
Air shaft
Dent Head Viaduct
Fell End Gill
waterfall
Koka Firth
Wold Fell
Newby Head Farm
Newby Head Gate
Blea Moor Hill
Dales Way
Coal Road
Monkey Beck
N
½
550
558
550
500
450
400
350
300
250
600
650
550

L12. Dent to Ribblehead *via the Ribble Way* (Maps 12, 12b & 8)

12.9 miles *(20.7 km)*   Ascent: 520m   Time: 6:15   (Strenuous)

(Alternative via Blea Moor: 9.3 miles (15.0 km)   Ascent: 290m   Time: 4:30   Moderate)

A long but fascinating high level walk following the River Ribble to its source high on Cam Fell.

*The Ribble Way starts (or finishes) high on Cam Fell at Gavel Gap, where a trickle begins, growing to become Jam Sike, merging into Long Gill, Gayle Beck and finally the River Ribble. The Ribble Way follows the new Pennine Bridleway west to Newby Head, along the Dent Road before turning south to follow the old trade route along Black Rake Road to **Gearstones**.*

This link walk follows the route of Walk 12 *(map 12)* from Dent Station, taking the drove road alternative around the flank of Great Knoutberry to drop to Newby Head Gate *(onto map 12b)*.

*Here there's an option: the short route bears right along the Dent Road for a quarter of a mile to follow the Ribble Way (& Dales Way) south across Blea Moor, above the meadows of High Gayle and Winshaw and down to **Gearstones**; the main route turns left along the Dent Road following the Ribble Way back up to its start on Cam Fell.*

The main route is easy to follow, across the busy B6255 and up along the **Pennine Bridleway** for **Cold Keld Gate**. Beyond the gate at Gavel Gap the grassy track rises to turn east, with long views opening out to the north down Snaizeholme, eventually running alongside a wall on the right to a gate. Through this, turn sharp right at Cold Keld Gate and join Cam High Road *(Pennine Way and Pennine Bridleway)* heading south-west.

Winter view down Dentdale from the drove road across Knoutberry.

The Dales Way comes up from Cam Houses to join the Cam Road at a cairn. It's an easy walk with excellent views of the Ribblehead Viaduct and the Three Peaks. The Pennine Way and Bridleway turn off at Cam End *(with an option to extend the walk even further down to Horton-in-Ribblesdale)*, but the main route continues to cross Gayle Beck at a bridge, joining the busy B6255 near Gearstones *(onto map 8)*. There follows a long mile and a half of road walking to Ribblehead, using the grass verges where possible, taking great care of fast traffic.

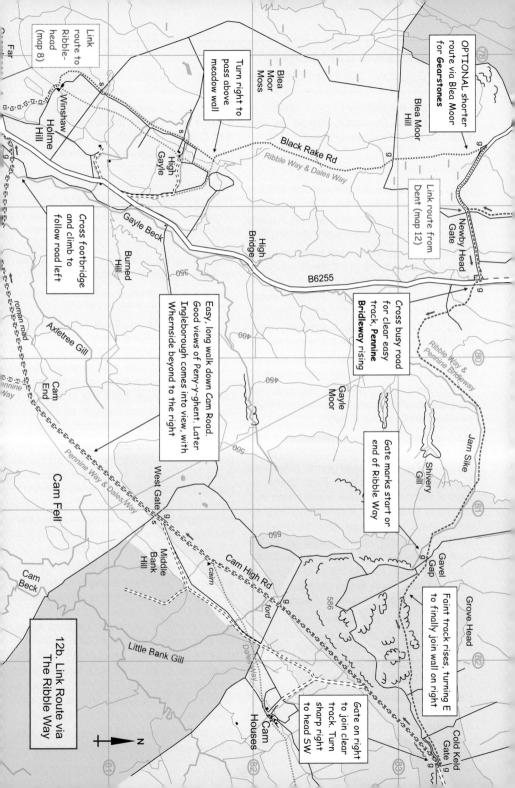

Blea Moor Moss

Blea Moor Hill

Turn right to pass above meadow wall

Black Rake Rd

Ribble Way & Dales Way

Link route to Ribblehead (map 8)

Link route from Dent (map 12)

Winshaw

Holme Hill

High Gayle

Newby Head Gate

Gayle Beck

High Bridge

Cross footbridge and climb to follow road left

Burned Hill

350

B6255

Cross busy road for clear easy track, **Pennine Bridleway** rising

Axletree Gill

roman road

400

Ribble Way & Pennine Bridleway

Cam End

Gayle Moor

450

Easy, long walk down Cam Road. Good views of Peny-y-ghent. Later Ingleborough comes into view, with Whernside beyond to the right

Shivery Gill

Jam Sike

Gate marks start or end of Ribble Way

500

Cam Fell

West Gate

Pennine Way & Dales Way

Middle Bank Hill

Cam High Rd

550

586

Gavel Gap

Grove Head

Faint track rises, turning E to finally join wall on right

Cam Beck

cairn

ford

Little Bank Gill

Dales Way

Cam Houses

Gate on right to join clear track. Turn sharp right to head SW

Cold Keld Gate

12b. Link Route via The Ribble Way

N

13. Garsdale & Dentdale

Dent / Garsdale   9.9 miles *(16.0 km)*   Time: 5:00   Ascent: 580m *Strenuous*

Explore the magnificent upper valleys of Garsdale and Dentdale, linked by the Coal Road and the Corpse Road.

Start at Dent Station for a circular walk, or Garsdale Station to finish at Dent (6.2 miles).

From Dent Station turn right up the Coal Road (1) to enjoy an exhilarating high level road walk along this quiet ancient route (2). A steep descent leads down to Garsdale Station (3).

By Garsdale Station turn left through a gate signed **FP Low Scale** (4). Cross a couple of fields to High Scale. Pass the old house and drop right, past a gate, down between stream and wall to a stile. Cross this and go over two fields until a barn below comes into view. Drop to pass behind this, out onto the road.

Cross the road to Low Scale farm (5), through a gate signed **FPs Old Road or Grouse Hall**. Go into the farmyard and turn left, through a couple of gates to cross a wooden footbridge over the fledgling River Clough.

Turn left and climb up the bank on the right (6) and cross the field diagonally towards some houses ahead. A couple of narrow stiles lead to the front of the cottages. Pass directly in front of them through three small gates and out onto a field. Continue ahead crossing two fields. Pass to the right of a barn before veering diagonally right to climb up to the road at the far corner gate. Turn left and walk down Old Road (7). Join the main Sedbergh road and walk down, taking care as it can be quite busy, to enter the hamlet at Garsdale.

Garsdale is the name of the narrow valley. There is really no village of that name, the houses being strung along its length, with the main cluster just up from the mid-19th century church of St John the Baptist .

Head straight down to Dandra Garth *(or take an optional route across the bridge for **Smarthwaite**, following the track above the river to recross at the road bridge and return* along **the Street** to Dandra Garth). Go through the gate at Dandra Garth marked **BW Cowgill** (8). Pass through the yard to another gate at the foot of a steep enclosed wooded track and begin the climb.

Pass through a gate out onto the open fell (9). This is a very boggy, steep section. The track curves left following the wall, before veering right to cross Blea Gill, climbing with the wall on the left. *Excellent long views open up and down Garsdale.* Where the ground begins to level out, the wall on the left becomes a fence.

*Beyond, in the distance on the left, the round turret of an air shaft marks the line of Rise Hill railway tunnel below. An archaeological dig by Channel 4's **Time Team** in 2008 – "the most exposed site Time Team has ever dug on" - investigated one of the smaller Victorian shanty towns set up for the navvies who dug the tunnel between 1869 and 1875. One of the five huts was excavated, as well as a boiler house and various workshops.*

The track now crosses a boggy section, but some board walks and flags help across the worst bits (10). The track veers right, away from the fence at a corner, heading south to meet a wall corner on the right. *(Ignore a stile on the right which gives access to a faint track heading west to cross the entire ridge of Rise Hill - an excellent walk in its own right.)*

Follow the wall on your right south to a gate by a forest. Through here a deeply rutted walled track (11) leads past the forest, where the view up Dentdale opens out on the left. *The station master's house can be seen across the deep ravine of Cowgill Beck.* The walled track leads down to a gate at a left bend, then steeply on down to Dockra Bridge, which crosses Cowgill Beck. *This track is known by some locally as the **Corpse Road**.* Follow the lane down to the road by St John's Church.

Turn left along the road (12) to Lea Yeat. Go left up the steep Coal Road to Dent Station.

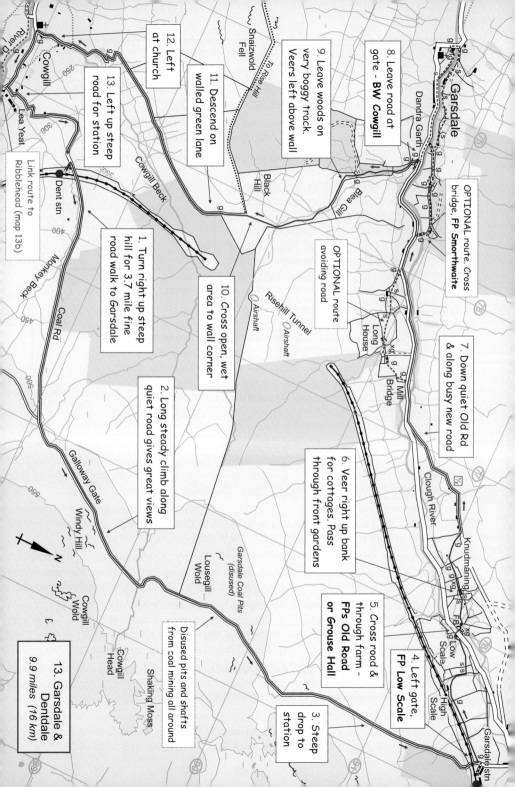

13. Garsdale & Dentdale
9.9 miles (16 km)

Link route to Ribblehead (map 13b)

1. Turn right up steep hill for 3.7 mile fine road walk to Garsdale

2. Long steady climb along quiet road gives great views

3. Steep drop to station

4. Left gate, **FP Low Scale**

5. Cross road & through farm - **FPs Old Road or Grouse Hall**

6. Veer right up bank for cottages. Pass through front gardens

7. Down quiet Old Rd & along busy new road

8. Leave road at gate - **BW Cowgill**

9. Leave woods on very boggy track. Veers left above wall

10. Cross open, wet area to wall corner

11. Descend on walled green lane

12. Left at church

13. Left up steep road for station

OPTIONAL route, avoiding road

OPTIONAL route. Cross bridge, **FP Smorthwaite**

Disused pits and shafts from coal mining all around

N

To Rise Hill

Snaizwold Fell

Black Hill

Blea Gill

Dandra Garth

Garsdale

Long House

Mill Bridge

Risehill Tunnel

Airshaft

Airshaft

Clough River

Knudmaning

Low Scale

High Scale

Garsdale stn

Garsdale Coal Pits (disused)

Lousegill Wold

Cowgill Head

Shaking Moss

Cowgill Wold

Windy Hill

Galloway Gate

Coal Rd

Monkey Beck

Dent stn

Cowgill Beck

Lea Yeat

Cowgill

River D

250

300

200

350

400

450

500

550

L13. Dent to Ribblehead, *via the Dales Way & Dales High Way*   (Maps 13, 13b & 9)

9.9 miles (*15.9 km*)   Time: 5:00   Ascent: 520m   (Strenuous)

Follow the Dales Way down Dentdale, and climb from Deepdale over the northern flank of Whernside on the route of A Dales High Way.

From Dent Station *(map 13)* turn left down the steep Coal Road to the cluster of houses at Lea Yeat, the largest settlement in the parish of Cowgill. Cross the bridge and turn right to join the riverside path to **Ewgales Bridge** following the Dales Way *(onto map 13b). The Dales Way is one of England's most popular long-distance trails. For over 50 years walkers have followed the 80 miles of riverside path from Ilkley, through the heart of the Yorkshire Dales to the foothills of southern Lakeland .*

Emerge by the bridge and continue west on the back road to Dent. After a quarter of a mile take a gate on the left for **Laithbank**, to pass below the farmhouse at Rivling and across a plantation to Little Town. Continue through the plantation beyond, following the contour to pass below Hackergill, across fields, joining a lane up to a fine house at Coat Faw. A gate on the right leads diagonally across a field to continue above a wall, around the back of a house at Clint, dropping below West Clint and on to Laithbank. The Dales Way now turns down the access lane to the road.

Go west along the road to a gate on the right opposite Tub Hole and drop to cross the River Dee at a footbridge. Now follow the river downstream to Tommy Bridge where you re-cross. Turn right, through a gate and on to climb a stile to the left of another gate. Follow the wall on your right, climbing straight on to cross a hill and rejoin the road at Bridge End.

There's an option here to continue to Dent, 1½ miles further west, taking about 40 minutes. Turn right over the bridge and pick up the footpath to **Church Bridge** *alongside Deepdale Beck, shared by both the Dales Way and Dales High Way. Return the same way.*

Otherwise, turn left and follow the road SE up to a junction by an old chapel, along the route of *A Dales High Way*. A more challenging route, it runs for 90 miles from the World Heritage village of Saltaire across the glorious high country of the Yorkshire Dales to Appleby-in-Westmorland.

Turn right up the steep narrow lane for 250 metres to a lane cutting off to the left marked *Craven Way, Public Bridleway, Ribblehead*. The clear track begins to climb quite steeply, with increasingly excellent long views back of Dentdale, the Howgills and the distant Lakeland Fells beyond. Eventually the path levels and passes through a gate onto open fell again.

There is an option here to head SSW for the summit of Whernside, climbing alongside the wall and continuing, where the wall drops away, towards the left of two prominent cairns, over wet ground to pass Whernside Tarns. Cross a stile onto the final ascent leg of Walk 9.

Otherwise, continue SE along a fine, green track, swinging south to pass a ruin. Whernside and Ingleborough dominate the view ahead *(onto map 9)*. The path begins to descend, through a gate to follow a wall on the left, joining the route of Walk 9 in reverse, to Ribblehead Station.

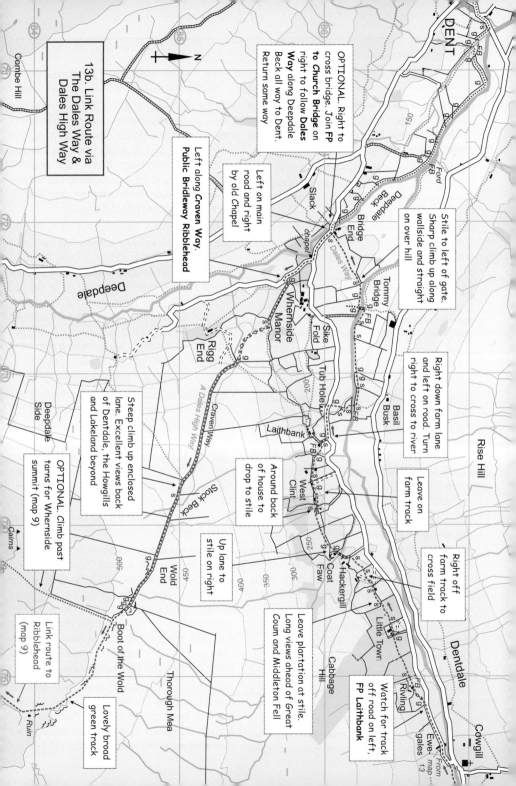

14. Cotterdale & Yoredale

Garsdale   **9.4 miles** *(15.1 km)*   Time: **4:45**   Ascent: **570m**   *Strenuous*

A fine high level walk from the deserted chapel at Lunds along the old corpse way to the secluded valley of Cotterdale, with magnificent long views into Wensleydale.

From Garsdale Station head down the road and go right at the junction for 250 metres, taking the stile on the left for **South Lunds** (1). Climb north to cross the rough pasture of Garsdale Low Moor, with excellent views of Dandrymire and Lunds Viaducts, dropping to cross the railway (2) and out onto the B6259.

Follow the road left past Quarry Farm to a stile for **Lunds** (3 - *the more direct route for High Dyke crosses boggy ground*). Cross a couple of fields diagonally to enter Lunds plantation at a field corner. The way through is well marked. Join the plantation track down to cross a footbridge to the tiny hamlet, taking a gate, right, into the church grounds (4).

Lunds Church was built as a single storey chapel-of-ease during the 18th century and the bench seats and altar rail date from this time. The church is surrounded by the small rounded glacial hills known as drumlins. The route over from Cotterdale was one along which the dead were carried to the tiny church - hence it is known as the corpse way.

Cross back over a footbridge for **Shaws** (5), passing in front of an old farmhouse and climbing straight up to pass above the former youth hostel, with its fine waterfall. Follow the wall above Shaws, bearing right to climb up onto the High Way (6). Take this southwest to the old ruined drovers' inn at High Dyke.

A choice here – either take the main route into Cotterdale, or continue along the High Way , for a shorter route cutting half a mile, easier underfoot, with excellent long views.

Turn left, climbing away from the wall along a faint track (7), sometimes wet underfoot, up to the ridge at Tarn Hill, with excellent views of Cotterdale ahead and Great Shunner Fell beyond. Continue due east, dropping to cross

into the plantation at a stile (8 - *the plantation road can be followed down into Cotterdale in mist*). The track drops steeply through the forest, much of it recently felled, to join the young Cotterdale Beck at West Gill. Look for some obvious stepping stones to the left (9), or use the bridge upstream if needed. Follow the beckside down into Cotterdale.

Cotterdale is the name given to both this quiet, secluded valley and the small hamlet of 13 properties it shelters. A survey of 1603 shows six titled wealthy men lived here, their family names later appearing in a rhyme: "Three Halls, two Kirks and a King. Same road out as goes in." In the early 19th century the hamlet supported a population of 100, engaged in farming, hand knitting and coal mining on the slopes of Great Shunner Fell.

Take the path on the right of the beck, climbing up to cross the road. Continue along a clear track for **Thwaite Bridge** (10), to reach the High Way above Cotter Riggs, with magnificent views into Upper Wensleydale.

Until the 18th century Wensleydale was also known as Yoredale (after the River Ure), and the geological strata of banded limestones, sandstones and shales that characterise the valley were given the name Yoredale Series by geologist John Phillips in 1835.

Continue southwest descending to Thwaite Bridge, turning right to pass the farm (11) and join an easy path beneath Cotter Side above the young River Ure (12). Finally pass through the farmyard at Yore House (13), cross the Ure by the waterfalls of Ure Force and take the path up to the Moorcock Inn. Give yourself 30 minutes for the final climb along the Pennine Bridleway to the station.

With careful planning, the walk can be extended from Cotterdale, taking the left bank of the beck to join the Pennine Way across Bluebell Hill and on to Hawes via Hardraw, returning to Garsdale on the bus.

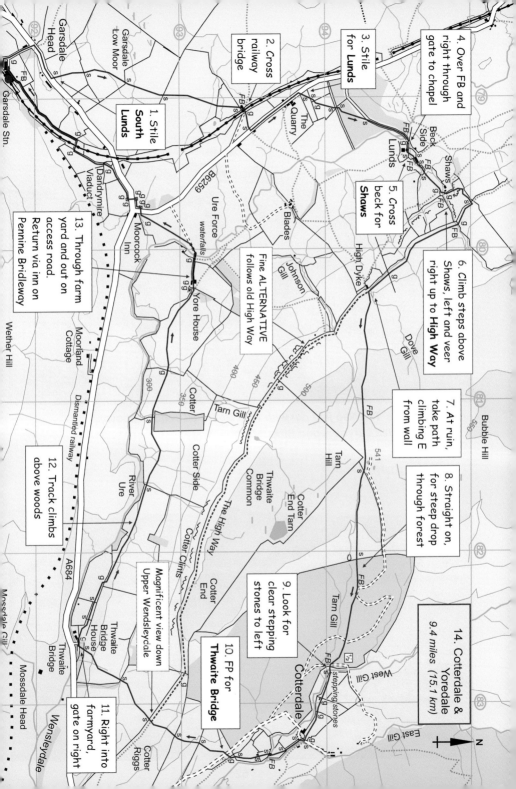

1. Stile South Lunds

2. Cross railway bridge

3. Stile for Lunds

4. Over FB and right through gate to chapel

5. Cross beck for Shaws

6. Climb steps above Shaws, left and veer right up to High Way

7. At ruin, take path climbing E from wall

8. Straight on, for steep drop through forest

9. Look for clear stepping stones to left

10. FP for Thwaite Bridge

11. Right into farmyard, gate on right

12. Track climbs above woods

13. Through farm yard and out on access road. Return via inn on Pennine Bridleway

14. Cotterdale & Yoredale 9.4 miles (15.1 km)

Fine ALTERNATIVE follows old High Way

Magnificent view down Upper Wensleydale

N

The Nab juts out with Wild Boar Fell behind (above)
The River Eden curves round Birkett Common at the foot of Mallerstang (below)

Walkers on the High Way (top left)
Ruins of Lammerside Castle (above)
Smardalegill Viaduct (top right)
Lunds Church (right)
River Eden at Stenkrith (below)

SECTION FOUR: Kirkby Stephen & Mallerstang

From Garsdale Head, the railway line goes north down the spectacular valley of Mallerstang, with the high, craggy escarpment of Mallerstang Edge to the east and the towering presence of Wild Boar Fell to the west. The line reaches its highest point at Aisgill Summit, then begins the long descent into the lush Eden Valley. Just to ride up and down the line here is a sheer delight.

At the foot of Mallerstang and the head of the broad Eden Valley sits the market town of Kirkby Stephen. The town was a key rural trading town and droving centre, receiving its first market charter in 1353, but as a former border town it suffered from the unwelcome attention of Scots raiders.

The earthworks called Croglam Castle at the southern end of town hint at prehistoric occupation, but the town itself grew as a Danish settlement in the 10th century, its name being recorded as **Cherkaby Stephen** in 1090. The parish church, built of soft red sandstone, is known locally as *the Cathedral of the Dales* and parts survive from the 12th century. Inside, the fascinating Loki Stone provides a link to the town's Viking origins, and there are monuments to important local families, including the Whartons and Musgraves. Access is from Market Square, through the Cloisters, built in 1810.

Around Kirkby Stephen the limestone beds of the Dales begin to dip under the later Permian red sandstones which give the buildings of the Eden Valley their characteristic colour. Where the two meet, a curious local stone known as Brockram is formed from an amalgam of limestone fragments embedded in a sandstone cement. This can be seen in the river beds at Stenkrith Park and in the walls of many of the buildings in town.

In 1857 work began on a major railway link between Darlington and the west coast. The Stainmore Railway opened in 1861, followed shortly by a connection north to Penrith. In 1875 the Settle-Carlisle line came, stopping at the new Kirkby Stephen West station a mile to the south. By the end of the 19th century more than a million tons of mineral freight was being hauled across Stainmore each year, and the railway had become the town's major employer. But in 1962 the Stainmore line closed and the track was quickly dismantled.

In 1989 the victory of the Friends of the Settle-Carlisle Line against its proposed closure gave impetus to a campaign to save Smardale Gill Viaduct, which faced demolition. Three years later the viaduct was restored, and the Northern Viaduct Trust established, which soon added the eastern Merrygill and Podgill Viaducts to its assets. With further land along the track secured by Cumbria Wildlife Trust and the John Strutt Conservation Foundation, much of the trackbed from Ravenstonedale to Stain Bank is now open for walkers to enjoy. Gaps remain, but campaigners are confident these problems will be resolved. These are, however, permissive routes, not rights of way, so access could be removed in the future.

Meanwhile railway enthusiasts have bought and restored the old Kirkby Stephen East railway station (open weekends) and have begun to restore track that they hope will one day see a heritage railway link up to Appleby.

The mainline station is 1½ miles from the town centre, reached by walking south up the main A685, past the caravan park, taking the lane on the left up to Halfpenny House, then joining the new Station Walk footpath to the station. The Black Bull Nateby Inn at Nateby is the nearest pub to the station, but you need to allow a good half hour to get your train.

Kirkby Stephen is a **Walkers are Welcome** town and has all the facilities a walker needs, including several fine pubs and cafes and plenty of accommodation, including a hostel. It was one of Alfred Wainwright's favourite Pennine towns and his much-loved Coast to Coast route passes through, crossing Smardale Fell from the west into town and leaving through Hartley on the way up to Nine Standards Rigg and on into Swaledale.

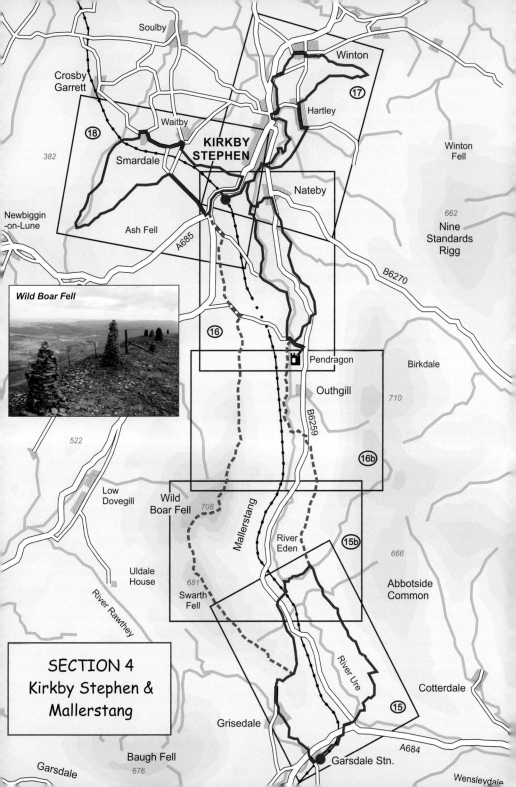

Soulby

Winton

Crosby
Garrett

(17)

Hartley

Waitby

Winton
Fell

(18)

**KIRKBY
STEPHEN**

382

Smardale

Nateby

662

Nine
Standards
Rigg

Newbiggin
-on-Lune

Ash Fell

A685

B6270

Wild Boar Fell

(16)

Pendragon

Birkdale

Outhgill

710

522

B6259

(16b)

Low
Dovegill

Wild
Boar Fell

708

Mallerstang

Uldale
House

River
Eden

(15b)

666

Abbotside
Common

681

Swarth
Fell

River Ure

Cotterdale

(15)

**SECTION 4
Kirkby Stephen &
Mallerstang**

Grisedale

A684

Baugh Fell

Garsdale Stn.

Garsdale

676

Wensleydale

15. Hellgill Force & the High Way

Garsdale   **8.8 miles** *(14.1 km)*   Time: **4:15**   Ascent: **400m**   *Moderate*

Explore the wild open fells at the head of Mallerstang, from the secluded valley of Grizedale to the beauty of Hellgill Force, returning along Lady Anne's High Way.

Hellgill Force

From Garsdale station turn right down the road to the T-junction. Go through the gate opposite. Following a wall on the left, climb up to a stile to the right of a gate ahead (1).

Go straight on along a faint track, above the deep gill of Grizedale Beck on the left, to a stile above Clough Force. Head to a gate at the right of Blake Mire farmhouse (2). Pass through a stile to the left of a farm track, continue NW until Grizedale opens up below. Head downhill, left of a derelict farmstead (3).

Grizedale was once dubbed "the dale that died" as its hill farms gave way to the economic hardships of the early twentieth century. Fortunately, the decline has been reversed more recently as new people have discovered the pleasures of its seclusion.

Through a stile turn up the field and go on to pass to the left of the houses at Moor Rigg, onto the road (4). Turn up to pass East House. Zigzag up the road to the open moor. Go right along a track for 130m, then turn sharp left (5) by a blue marker post to climb straight up the fell side. There's no clear track here. As the ground levels near the ridge, head for a gate where the wall on the right meets a fence from the left and go through.

Follow the wall on your right downhill, veering away to head north (6), turning parallel with the road and railway below. There's no clear track. Head for a barn ruin which appears ahead. Beyond the barn follow the wall on the right, closing to the road, which you eventually join across a small footbridge (7).

At Ais Gill cottages, turn right down a lane to cross a bridge over the railway. Turn left and follow the road to a fork. The route goes right, up to Hellgill farm, but first cut to the left along a faint track to view Hellgill Force waterfall (8).

Return to the access road and head east, across a bridge and up through the farm. Pass between buildings, and continue up the narrow field to a stile beside a gate. Turn right to cross Hellgill Bridge (9) and follow the track SE, cutting left at a fork (10) on the *Pennine Bridleway* to climb gently above a walled enclosure, and on above intake walls (11).

Pass High Hall and go on, gently climbing, through a gate onto High Abbotside. Beyond the ruins of High Dyke, a former drovers' inn, cross a beck and look for a gate on the right leading onto the *Pennine Bridleway* (12).

The track drops downhill, swinging right to a gap where Johnston Gill is fenced off. Here bear sharp left (13) to join another beck on your left, following this down to a plantation. Bear right beside the plantation down to a gate, then left to cross a double bridge (14).

Follow the road a short way to where a track cuts off left, heading up to the Moorcock Inn.

The Pennine Bridleway leads over two roads through several gates, climbing to pass under the viaduct and alongside the railway up behind the railway cottages and out onto the road. Left and left again up to the station.

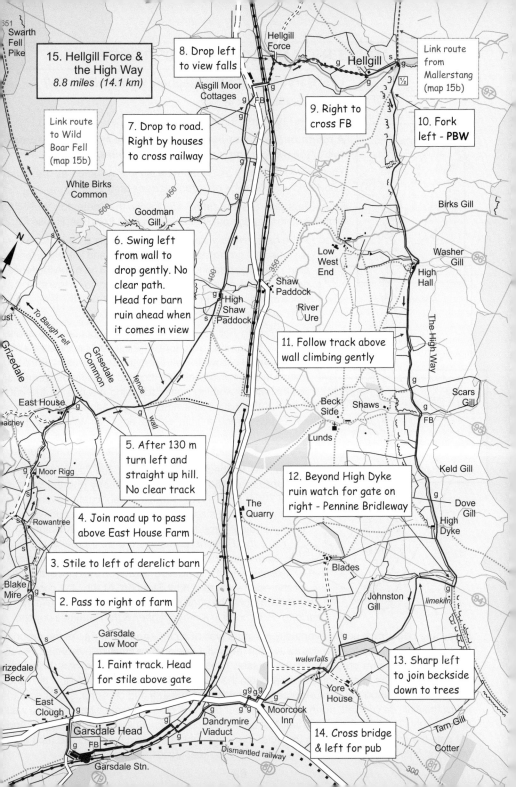

15. Hellgill Force & the High Way
8.8 miles (14.1 km)

Swarth Fell Pike

Hellgill Force

Hellgill

8. Drop left to view falls

Aisgill Moor Cottages

Link route from Mallerstang (map 15b)

9. Right to cross FB

10. Fork left - PBW

Link route to Wild Boar Fell (map 15b)

7. Drop to road. Right by houses to cross railway

White Birks Common

Birks Gill

Goodman Gill

Washer Gill

Low West End

High Hall

6. Swing left from wall to drop gently. No clear path. Head for barn ruin ahead when it comes in view

Shaw Paddock

High Shaw Paddock

River Ure

The High Way

11. Follow track above wall climbing gently

Grisedale Common

Scars Gill

East House

Beck Side

Shaws

FB

Lunds

Keld Gill

5. After 130 m turn left and straight up hill. No clear track

12. Beyond High Dyke ruin watch for gate on right - Pennine Bridleway

Dove Gill

Moor Rigg

The Quarry

High Dyke

4. Join road up to pass above East House Farm

Rowantree

3. Stile to left of derelict barn

Blake Mire

2. Pass to right of farm

Blades

Johnston Gill

limekiln

Garsdale Low Moor

13. Sharp left to join beckside down to trees

1. Faint track. Head for stile above gate

waterfalls

rizedale Beck

Yore House

East Clough

Garsdale Head

Dandrymire Viaduct

Moorcock Inn

14. Cross bridge & left for pub

Tarn Gill

Cotter

FB

Dismantled railway

Garsdale Stn.

L15. Garsdale to Kirkby Stephen, *via Wild Boar Fell*
(Maps 15, 15b, 16b, 16)

KIRKBY
STEPHEN

Nateby

Stn.

16

Dalefoot

16b

Shoregill

L16

Wild
Boar
Fell

15b

Aisgill

Hellgill

L15

15

Grisedale

Garsdale

11.8 miles (*19.0 km*) Time: 5:45 Ascent: 620m (Strenuous)

A tough but exhilarating ridge walk above Mallerstang across two of the wildest and loneliest of the Pennine peaks.

This walk should only be undertaken in clear weather, as the route follows close to the edge of a precipitous escarpment.

From Garsdale Station *(map 15)* follow the route for Walk 15 climbing up to the ridge on Grisedale Common from East House (5).

Head for the gate where a wall on the right meets a fence from the left, but don't go through. Instead turn left and follow the fence along the ridge heading NW. Keep straight on when the fence dog-legs right, crossing a boggy patch and go on to a stile at a fence corner. Cross this and continue NW, with the fence now on your left to the summit of Swarth Fell Pike.

From Swarth Fell Pike *(onto map 15b)* continue to climb gently NW, parallel to the fence, which now becomes a wall, to the summit of Swarth Fell. From the summit cairn, the path rejoins the wall on the left and drops to a saddle between the peaks before climbing again, following a fence on the left. Halfway up the path veers right, rising diagonally across the Band. Finally reach a stile at the edge of Wild Boar Fell, overlooking the valley below. *The view across the valley is magnificent.* A number of cairns and a shelter stand on the edge.

Across a stile, the best route now follows the ridge edge to the Nab *(onto map 16b)*, which juts out clearly (the trig point is about 700m to the NW). From the Nab, continue along the edge above the steep scree slopes of the Scriddles, now descending. Drop to the wall corner at High Dolphinsty. *Here the Pennine Bridleway crosses, providing a fine alternative route into the valley if required.* Otherwise continue north following the track on the right of the wall for the ridge walk to Kirkby Stephen. At the wall corner go straight on along the ridge track to the brow of Little Fell. *There are long views north to Kirkby Stephen & the Pennines beyond.*

Follow the ridge track north, eventually joining a wall at a corner on the right. As the ground begins to level out, the track veers away from the wall, heading for a small hillock ahead. A wet area where a stream crosses is soon passed *(onto map 16)*. Beyond the next hillock at Greenlaw Rigg, the track begins to drop to join the Tommy Road. Turn left and follow the road to pass a lime kiln on the right. Approaching a wall with a cattle grid crossing, swing right to follow the wall, on your left, north. Eventually veer right and cross towards a barn to join a wall on your right. The track leaves the wall just before a second barn. Follow it through a gate and out onto the road. Turn left along the quiet road and right at the next junction. The next right takes you onto the busy A685 and down to the station keeping to the broad verge.

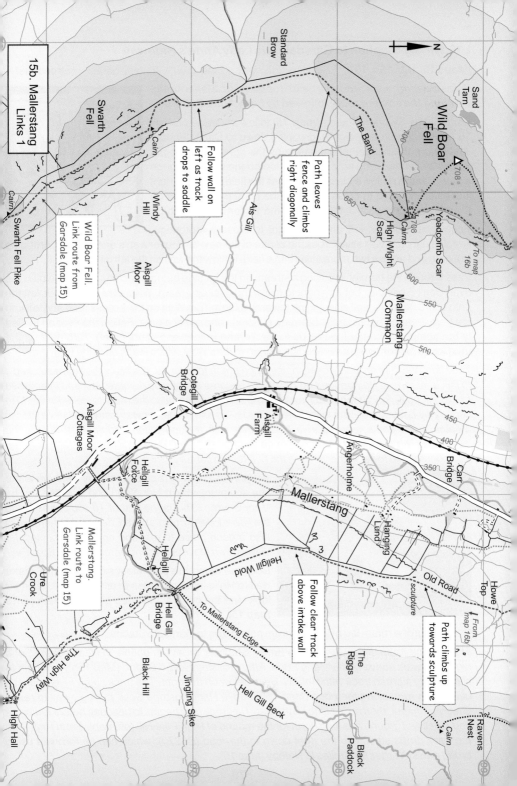

L16. Kirkby Stephen to Garsdale, *via Lady Anne's Highway*

(Maps 16, 16b, 15b, 15)   12.6 miles *(20.3 km)*   Time: 6:00   Ascent: 560m   (Strenuous)

A fascinating walk into the wild foothills of Mallerstang, climbing the ancient route followed by Lady Anne Clifford.

From Kirkby Stephen Station *(map 16)* follow the route of Walk 16 for Pendragon (to point 6), dropping down to Castle Bridge. Just before the bridge, take the gate on the right for **Shoregill**. Follow the fence on the right to cross a footbridge and on through a gate. Climb to follow a clear path across the field, swinging right just before the end to cross a stile on the right, then another on the left, and continue with the fence on the left *(onto map 16b)*.

Pass a barn on the left and drop right to cross a footbridge, keeping right to a wall stile. Cross the centre of the next field, over a stile and veer left, dropping to a gate and across two more stiles into a field. Follow the wall on the left into Shoregill.

Pass through the hamlet, crossing a stream on the far side before reaching the bridge over the river. Don't cross this, but turn right to follow the river upstream. Where the river bends left the path veers right to a wall stile and on towards a farm. Turn right on the access road and left into the farm, bearing right to pass between buildings and out at a gate. Follow the river on the left to the humpback bridge leading up to the Thrang (a former country hotel). Turn right up the road for 20 metres to a gate on the left, signed **Public Way**, which leads on to the High Way.

The High Way has probably been in use since prehistoric times. It is likely the Romans used it to link their forts at Bainbridge and Brough. It became a major packhorse trail, and later drove route, linking Kirkby Stephen to Hawes and Dentdale. It was also the route travelled in the 17th century by Lady Anne – the last of the Cliffords - as she made her way between her castles in Skipton and Penrith, carried in a horse-litter, with a huge coterie sometimes numbering hundreds. The High Way continued to be the main trading route until the new turnpike road was constructed lower in the valley in the nineteenth century.

Water Cut

(Map 15b) The way is clear, a steady climb up to the fine sculpture above Hanging Lund - **Water Cut** by Mary Bourne. *This is the first of 10 sculptures along the River Eden known as the Eden Benchmarks. It is also a good place to rest and enjoy the spectacular views down Mallerstang and across to Wild Boar Fell.*

Continue along the path alongside the upper intake wall to Hellgill Bridge. Pass over the bridge, taking a look over the edge at the deep gorge beneath *(onto map 15)*.

Now pick up the return leg of Walk 15 from point 10 on to Garsdale Station.

The reverse route, from Garsdale to Kirkby Stephen, gives the option, in clear weather, of a high level walk above Mallerstang Edge. After crossing Hellgill Bridge (Map 15b), turn right to climb along a green track with Hell Gill Beck below on the right. The track finally levels out at a cairn, then runs along the edge (Map 16b) above Hangingstone Scar, pulling away to reach Gregory Chapel, then on to climb High Seat. The track now begins to descend before fading as you cross wet ground heading north for the mound of High Pike Hill (off map). From High Pike the track drops steeply to the right down to the road (B6270), which can be followed using broad grassy verges for 3 miles to Nateby (Map 16).

16. Pendragon

Kirkby Stephen   8.3 miles *(13.4 km)*   Time: **4:00** Ascent: **330m** *Moderate*

A lovely, gentle walk into the open northern foothills of Mallerstang, steeped in late medieval history.

Take the footpath from the station for **Kirkby Stephen** (1). Turn right at Halfpenny House (2) and follow the road towards Wharton Hall. Leave the access road at a gate on the right, signed **Public bridleway, Wharton** (3) to climb above the farm buildings, before dropping left back towards the hall. Turn right to continue along the access road.

Wharton Hall is an impressive tower house, with a gatehouse, internal courtyard and out buildings dating from the 14th to the 17th century. Built by Sir Thomas Wharton, the hall is now part of a modern working farm.

Pass more farm buildings and Mire Close Bridge on your left. Go through a gate and turn left through another, leaving the access road. Follow the fence on the left above the river, heading south. Climb to a gate, where excellent long views up Mallerstang open. Go straight on to cross two fields (4) before the path climbs diagonally right and the remains of Lammerside Castle come into view.

Lammerside Castle, originally a 12th century building, was rebuilt in the 14th century as a Pele tower, to provide protection against Scots raiders. The castle was occupied by the Wharton family until the 17th century, when they abandoned it and moved to the fortified manor house at Wharton Hall.

Go past the ruins to a gate, turning sharp left (5) onto a byway beside the river. *Easy walking now on a clear green lane.* The path climbs gently with Birkett Common above on the right. Approaching above the impressive wooded Catagill Scar, the sharp escarpment of Mallerstang Edge dominates the view ahead on the left, with the point of the Nab on Wild Boar Fell rising to the right.

Reaching Tommy Road, turn left by a cattle grid (6). Follow the road down to cross Castle Bridge and on up to a road junction. A gate on the right gives access to Pendragon Castle.

Although local legend would have it that the castle was built by King Arthur's father Uther Pendragon, it was probably built in the 12th century by the Norman baron Ranulph de Meschines. Destroyed by a fire in 1541, it lay in ruins until Lady Anne Clifford rebuilt it in 1660. It remained one of her favourite castles until her death in 1676.

Return to the bridge (7), taking a stile on the right. Cross a small field to another stile, then climb diagonally right passing to the left of a barn. Continue in a straight line towards farm buildings and a gate at the far field corner, out onto the road. Turn left, then right up a farm lane - **Public Footpath Nateby** (9). Bear left before Southwaite Cottage and take the right of two gates, up the field with the beck on the right. Through a gate bear left, climbing above a barn to cross a deep gill and 2 stiles.

Continue on to a gate above Carr House. Another gate leads on to a stile, crossing above a wall into new woodland. Beyond a gate, where the wall drops left down to the river, go straight on (9), eventually joining a broad green track coming up from the left.

Join a wall coming up from the left towards the remains of Ridding House. Cross a stile in the corner and follow the track down between a crumbled wall on the left and a deep gill on the right. Pass through a gate and go straight on, until the wall on the left finally closes in to a footbridge over a beck to a gate (10). Veer left to cross the field to a gate, then straight on across two fields out onto the road.

Follow the road to Nateby (11). Watch for sign on the left marked **Public Footpath Wharton Hall** (12). Go along the track and cross three fields to drop to the river, following it left to cross a footbridge. Climb a field to a gate onto the Wharton Hall access road and turn right to retrace your route back to the station (13).

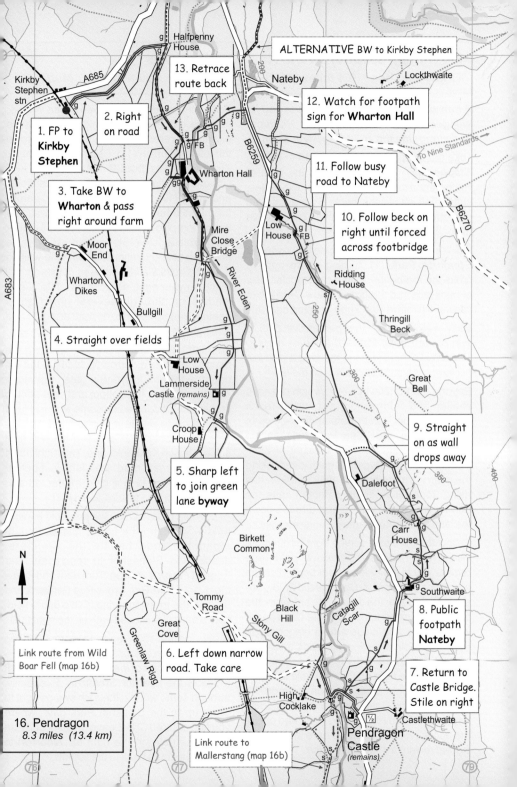

ALTERNATIVE BW to Kirkby Stephen

Halfpenny House

Lockthwaite

Nateby

A685

Kirkby Stephen stn

13. Retrace route back

12. Watch for footpath sign for **Wharton Hall**

1. FP to **Kirkby Stephen**

2. Right on road

Wharton Hall

11. Follow busy road to Nateby

B6259

To Nine Standards

B6270

3. Take BW to **Wharton** & pass right around farm

Mire Close Bridge

Low House

FB

10. Follow beck on right until forced across footbridge

Moor End

Wharton Dikes

River Eden

Ridding House

Thringill Beck

A683

Bullgill

4. Straight over fields

Low House

Lammerside Castle *(remains)*

Great Bell

9. Straight on as wall drops away

Croop House

5. Sharp left to join green lane **byway**

Dalefoot

Carr House

Birkett Common

N

Link route from Wild Boar Fell (map 16b)

Tommy Road

Great Cove

Greenlaw Rigg

Black Hill

Stony Gill

Catagill Scar

Southwaite

8. Public footpath **Nateby**

6. Left down narrow road. Take care

High Cocklake

7. Return to Castle Bridge. Stile on right

Castlethwaite

16. Pendragon
8.3 miles (13.4 km)

Pendragon Castle *(remains)*

Link route to Mallerstang (map 16b)

78   77   79

17. Kirkby Stephen & the Northern Viaducts

Kirkby Stephen   **9.4 miles** *(15.1 km)*   Time: **4:30**   Ascent: **390m**   *Moderate*

A fine walk around Kirkby Stephen and its villages, across the Northern Viaducts and alongside the sparkling River Eden .

Take the footpath from the station to **Kirkby Stephen** (1). Take the gate to the right of Halfpenny House (2) to cross two stiles, cutting left above the beck. By the caravan park drop right around a fenced bank above the beck (3) and up to the road by the bridge.

Go left on the road to a gate opposite for **Stenkrith Park** (4), turning sharp right to cross the footbridge, with a spectacular view of beck falls and the gorge below. Turn left to join the old railway trackbed heading east (5).

Easy walking now. This permissive path is part of the Poetry Path – 12 poems by Meg Peacocke carved in stone marking a year in a hill farmer's life. September is on the left.

Beyond the Platelayer's Hut, which provides shelter and information, you soon reach Podgill Viaduct – with outstanding views of the Pennines and Eden Valley 11 arches cross Ladthwaite Beck at a height of 26m. Further on is Merrygill Viaduct, overlooking the quarry, a more humble affair with 9 arches rising 24m above Hartley Beck. Leave the railway line by the quarry and turn left down the lane (6) to enter Hartley. Beware lorries.

Follow the road as it curves right through the village (*an optional permissive path here returns you to the railway trackbed*). Turn up a lane for **Whingill & Cotegarth** (7) to pass straight through the farm (8), between the buildings, and the left of two gates by a pencil wood. At the end cross a field diagonally to the right to join a track which runs under the railway embankment (9). Continue parallel to the wall on the right up the next field to a gate at the top right corner, and on towards the trees sheltering Cote Garth farmhouse. Pass through the yard (9), bearing right, and out on the access road. *The views here are lovely – a great reward for such little effort.*

Follow the road, left, between broad verges, past the old railway embankment where the permissive railway route ends. Take a gate on the left for **Winton** (11). Care is needed here. The path veers from the wall to drop in a straight line diagonally across several fields and stiles (12). In field three watch carefully for the stile halfway along the right wall. At the bottom, cross a stile in the left wall corner along from a gate (13). Turn left, cross a stile on the right and continue left with the wall on the left. Cross a stile and head uphill with the fence on your right, as it curves left to a gate leading on through several gated stiles behind Winton. Drop to the road at a gate and turn right up past the pub to the village green.

Turn left by the Manor House (14) along the main street, into a narrow footpath on the left near the far end. Beyond a gate drop along side the fence to the bottom and veer right to cross a footbridge beside some woods. Head straight up to a stile in a short wall section (15), and straight on crossing several field stiles to reach Kirkbank Lane. Turn right down to the busy main road, then left. Just before the road bridge take a gate on the left and cross a footbridge to join the river (16).

At Low Mill Bridge cross the river and explore Kirkby Stephen (17). Leave Market Square along the road beside the Cloisters, descending Stoneshot to reach the river Eden at **Frank's Bridge**. Turn right and follow the river to **Pod Gill**. Cross Pod Gill Beck and beyond the trees, ignoring a stile into a field, take a narrow enclosed path on the right (19).

A gate on the right leads to a track cutting back and down to cross Swingy Bridge (20) – *the start and end of the Poetry Path*. Turn left to follow the river for **Stenkrith**. Eventually, through some woods, the path swings right to climb up to the Stenkrith Park gate, where you first entered (21). Leave the park and turn left to the gate on the right for **Wharton** to retrace the route back to the station.

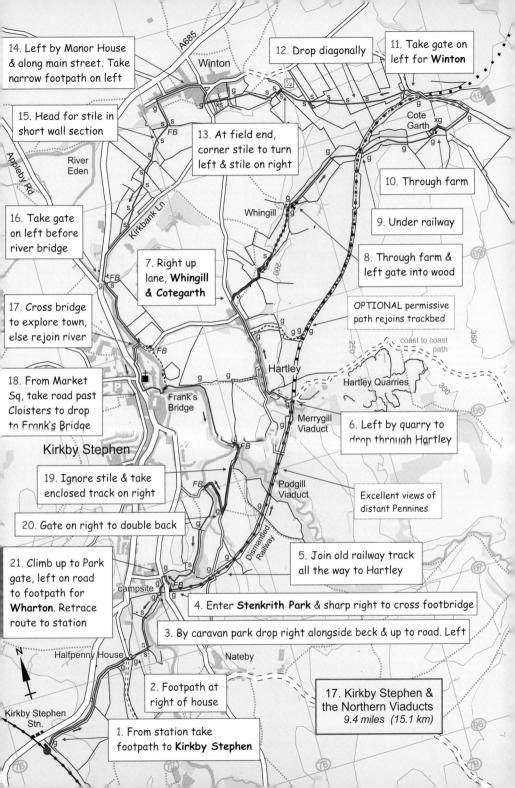

14. Left by Manor House & along main street. Take narrow footpath on left

12. Drop diagonally

11. Take gate on left for **Winton**

Winton

A685

15. Head for stile in short wall section

13. At field end, corner stile to turn left & stile on right

Cote Garth

10. Through farm

River Eden

Whingill

9. Under railway

16. Take gate on left before river bridge

7. Right up lane, **Whingill & Cotegarth**

8. Through farm & left gate into wood

Appleby Rd

Kirkbank Ln

OPTIONAL permissive path rejoins trackbed

coast to coast path

17. Cross bridge to explore town, else rejoin river

FB

Hartley

18. From Market Sq, take road past Cloisters to drop to Frank's Bridge

P

Frank's Bridge

Hartley Quarries

Merrygill Viaduct

6. Left by quarry to drop through Hartley

Kirkby Stephen

Excellent views of distant Pennines

19. Ignore stile & take enclosed track on right

FB

Podgill Viaduct

20. Gate on right to double back

Dismantled Railway

5. Join old railway track all the way to Hartley

21. Climb up to Park gate, left on road to footpath for **Wharton**. Retrace route to station

campsite

FB

4. Enter **Stenkrith Park** & sharp right to cross footbridge

3. By caravan park drop right alongside beck & up to road. Left

N

Halfpenny House

Nateby

2. Footpath at right of house

17. Kirkby Stephen & the Northern Viaducts
9.4 miles (15.1 km)

Kirkby Stephen Stn.

1. From station take footpath to **Kirkby Stephen**

18. Smardale

Kirkby Stephen   **8.5 miles** *(13.6 km)*   Time: **4:00** Ascent: **390m**   *Moderate*

A beautiful, airy walk through Smardale nature reserve along the disused Stainmore railway line to cross Smardale Viaduct, returning over Smardale Fell.

From the station, turn right down the very busy A685 main road towards town, taking great care of the fast moving traffic (1). Take the footpath on the left for **Ashfell** (2), through a gate to enter a green lane. (*A safer, option is to take the Station Walk footpath, joining the road halfway down through two gates, though not strictly a right of way. Otherwise continue for **Kirkby Stephen** and join the route via the Coast to Coast path*).

Pass a splendid example of a lime kiln, with nice open views of the Pennines. Continue through a gate with a wall/fence on the left to a stile into a copse. Leave the copse and follow the fence on the left up to a wall stile.

Head straight forward over the field towards a railway underpass (3), but don't go through. Instead, turn sharp right to a gate and head diagonally up and across the field to drop to a gate in the far right corner onto the road. Turn right on the road, and left at the junction, then left again along the road to **Smardale** (*there's an option here to turn right through the small hamlet of Waitby, following a track to join the undeveloped railway trackbed early, on a permissive path*). Ignore a left turn by the old school and go on to pass the turnoff to Smardale itself (4).

The tiny village of Smardale is dominated by Smardale Hall which dates from the 15th and 16th century The current west wing is marked by four conical round towers. It was built on the site of an older fortification - there are the remains of a motte and ditch to the north.

Pass the former Station House on your left to cross the old railway bridge. Turn left and left again between houses to enter the nature reserve at a gate. *A National Nature Reserve since 1997, it occupies a 3.5 mile section of*

the disused railway and is owned and managed by the Cumbria Wildlife Trust. The steep wooded slopes of Smardale Gill, carved by Scandal Beck, harbour abundant wildflowers like knapweed and scabious, and are a haven for butterflies such as the Scotch argus, seen here at its southernmost limit.*

Follow this permissive path under Smardale Viaduct, which carries the Settle-Carlisle line, at a gate and continue along the disused railway (7). As you approach the awesome Smardalegill Viaduct, the views open out. Through another gate pass an old quarry and double lime kilns. Just beyond the railway cottages pass under a bridge and turn left, climbing to cross a stile and follow the track right, now on the Coast to Coast path (8).

Drop to cross Smardale Bridge, through a gate and up the other side on a wide track between walls, heading east for **Kirkby Stephen** (9). Beyond two more gates pass a wall corner and continue parallel to the wall on the left heading NE over Smardale Fell.

At the next wall corner continue straight on, along the right of several tracks, rising (10). Eventually over the brow a wall comes up from the left. Join it and follow it down. *There are great views of the Pennines and Mallerstang, with Wild Boar Fell on the right.*

Through a gate turn right onto the quiet road (11 - *if returning to Kirkby Stephen, take the next left and cross a stile on your right, following the Coast to Coast path back*). Turn left at Lane Head and left again onto the main A685 road (12). Follow it with great care, using the wide verges, down to the station.

Note: *To start from Kirkby Stephen Market Square, head west through one of the many ginnels onto Faraday Rd. Follow it left to West Garth and continue along a narrow back lane (Croglam Lane) behind the houses to join the Coast to Coast path. Follow this to join the main route just beyond the copse (3).*

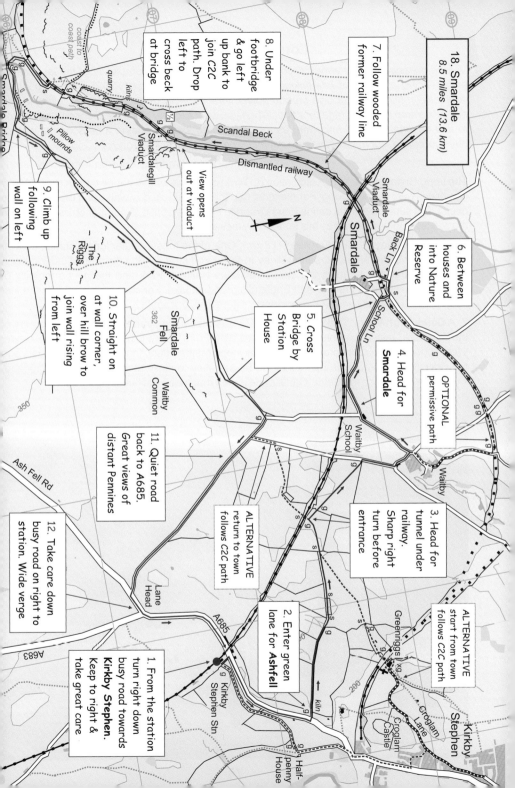

18. Smardale
8.5 miles (13.6 km)

7. Follow wooded former railway line

8. Under footbridge & go left up bank to join C2C path. Drop left to cross beck at bridge

Scandal Beck

Smardalegill Viaduct

Dismantled railway

View opens out at viaduct

Smardale Viaduct

Smardale

6. Between houses and into Nature Reserve

Back Ln

School Ln

9. Climb up following wall on left

The Riggs

Pillow mounds

quarry

kilns

coast to coast path

Smardale Bridge

Smardale Fell

362

350

Waitby Common

10. Straight on at wall corner, over hill brow to join wall rising from left

5. Cross Bridge by Station House

4. Head for **Smardale**

OPTIONAL permissive path

Waitby School

Waitby

3. Head for tunnel under railway. Sharp right turn before entrance

11. Quiet road back to A685. Great views of distant Pennines

Ash Fell Rd

Lane Head

ALTERNATIVE return to town follows C2C path

12. Take care down busy road on right to station. Wide verge

A685

2. Enter green lane for **Ashfell**

ALTERNATIVE start from town follows C2C path

Greenriggs

Croglam Castle

Croglam Lane

Kirkby Stephen

A683

1. From the station turn right down busy road towards **Kirkby Stephen.** Keep to right & take great care

Kirkby Stephen Stn

kiln

Half-penny House

Long Distance Trails

"A long distance walk is about discovering the true scale and complexity of the landscape, experiencing a sense of interlinking places. It's also about discovering something about yourself – relying on your own muscle power, your capacity of endurance, achieving longer distances step by step, stage by stage. When you walk a longer distance, the means of getting to that destination is as important as the destination itself, a goal in a personal as well as physical sense. For most of us, it is an achievement we are rightly proud of."

– Colin Speakman, ***Walk!*** (Great Northern Books, 2011)

The Long Distance Walkers Association (LDWA) defines a long distance trail, in the main, as one that is over 20 miles long. For the most part these are multi-day walks and the LDWA lists over 1,600 such trails in its online Long Distance Paths database. A number cross the area of the western Dales covered by this book. They include:

1. **The Dales Way** (1969) 80 miles (*128 km*). One of the most popular long distance trails, it mainly follows riverside paths from Ilkley in West Yorkshire to Bowness-on-Windermere. It passes through the heart of the Yorkshire Dales National Park and the gentle foothills of Southern Lakeland to the shore of England's grandest lake. For many people this is the first long distance trail they undertake, and many return to walk it again.

2. **A Dales High Way** (2008) 90 miles (*145 km*). A challenging trail across the high country of the Yorkshire Dales, it complements the Dales Way. From the world heritage village of Saltaire, West Yorkshire, the route crosses Rombalds Moor, Malhamdale, Ingleborough, Dentdale and the Howgill Fells before dropping into the Eden Valley to finish at Appleby-in-Westmorland. The return journey on the Settle-Carlisle line is very much a part of the experience.

Members of Swaledale Outdoor Club head for Crummackdale, on A Dales High Way 2011.
Photo (c) Barbara Gravenor

3. **A Coast to Coast Walk** (1973) 190 miles (*306 km*). Alfred Wainwright's classic walk from the west coast to the east is the most popular of all the long distance trails. From St Bees in Cumbria it crosses the Lake District National Park, the Eden Valley at Kirkby Stephen, the Yorkshire Dales National Park, the Vale of York and the North York Moors National Park to finish at Robin Hoods Bay.

4. **The Pennine Way** (1965) 268 miles (*429 km*). The very first of the national trails, opened after a 30-year campaign by its founder Tom Stephenson. It's a tough route following the central upland spine of England from Edale in the Peak District National Park, north through the Yorkshire Dales, along Hadrians Wall and north across the Cheviots to the Scottish border, finishing at Kirk Yetholm.

5. **The Pennine Bridleway** (2002 -?) When complete it will cover 347miles (*558 km*) from Middleton Top, Derbyshire to Byrness, Northumberland. The newest of the national trails, currently 205 miles (*330 km*) are open as far north as Street, Ravenstonedale.

6. **The Ribble Way** (1985) 65 miles (*105 km*). It follows the route of the River Ribble from the river mouth at Longton in Lancashire to its source on Gayle Moor, passing Preston, Ribchester, Clitheroe, Settle and Horton-in-Ribblesdale.

7. **Lady Anne's Way** (1995) 100 miles (*161 km*). Based loosely on the travels of the remarkable Lady Anne Clifford as she visited her various holdings in the early 17th century. It takes in Skipton Castle, Barden Tower (Wharfedale), Nappa Hall (Wensleydale), Pendragon Castle (Mallerstang), Brough Castle, Appleby Castle and Brougham Castle at Penrith.

8. **The Settle - Carlisle Wa**y (2005) 97 mile (*156 km*). A version first appeared in 1980, but the current route follows public footpaths along the length of the line, linking stations from Settle to Carlisle.

9. **A Pennine Journey** (2010) 247 miles (*398 km*). Based loosely on a long, solitary walk of self discovery made by the young Alfred Wainwright in 1938, it's a circular route from Settle to Hadrian's Wall and back, going north along the eastern Pennines and returning along the western Pennines.

10. **The Yoredale Way** (1980) 100 miles (*161 km*). It runs from York to Kirkby Stephen following the River Ure through Wensleydale, passing Boroughbridge, Ripon, Masham, Middleham, Askrigg and Hawes.

And finally, **the Six Peaks Trail** (2012), see over ......

Walkers on a FoSCL guided walk using a new section of the Pennine Bridleway by Garsdale Station.

The Six Peaks Trail

Settle to Kirkby Stephen

48.4 miles (*77.9 km*)

Ascent: 3050 m

The Six Peaks Trail is a long distance walk of 48 miles which follows the line of the railway from Settle to Kirkby Stephen. As the name suggests, it takes in six peaks: Pen-y-ghent, Ingleborough, Whernside, Great Knoutberry, Swarth Fell and Wild Boar Fell.

The route divides into four sections and for those wishing to walk it in one go, accommodation can be found at Horton-in-Ribblesdale, Ribblehead and Garsdale.

Each section ends at a railway station so the trail can be easily tackled in stages, using the train to get to and from a base. Settle, in particular, with its excellent facilities and easy access to the station, makes a great base for a long distance walk like this.

This is a challenging route with a total ascent of 3,050 metres. In mountain-bagging parlance, all six peaks are Nuttalls and Hewitts, and all but Swarth Fell are Marilyns. The landscape is exposed and good, clear weather is a must for this walk. The instructions suggest alternative routes for bad weather conditions.

The Six Peaks Trail was constructed by linking other routes in this book.

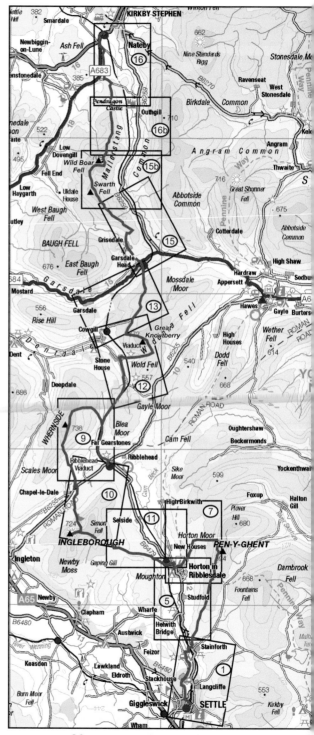

Stage 1: Settle to Horton-in-Ribblesdale *(Maps 1, 5 & 7)*

11.3 miles (*18.2 km*)   Ascent: 680 m   Time: 5:45 hrs

From Settle Station follow Linear Link Route L1, taking the option to climb Pen-y-ghent.

(Map 1) The route follows the Ribble Way north through Stainforth *(onto map 5)*, climbing up to Moor Head Lane. (*In bad weather, drop to Helwith Bridge to follow the riverbank to Horton.*) Continue north on the track signed *FP Long Lane (onto map 7)*, dipping to Churn Milk Hole to pick up the Pennine Way for the summit of Pen-y-ghent. From the summit, follow the return route of Walk 7 down along Horton Scar Lane to Horton-in-Ribblesdale.

Stage 2: Horton-in-Ribblesdale to Ribblehead *(Maps 11, 10 & 9)*

14.0 miles (*22.5 km*)   Ascent: 1020 m   Time: 7:15 hrs

From Horton-in-Ribblesdale the way follows the popular Three Peaks Challenge Route in reverse to Ribblehead, crossing Ingleborough and Whernside.

(Map 11) Take the route of Walk 11 in reverse, heading west along the popular Three Peaks path, past the shooting hut *(onto map 10)* for the summit of Ingleborough. Retrace your steps from the summit, keeping left at a fork in the slabbed descent path, for a very steep descent to Humphrey Bottom (best avoided in icy conditions). Head north to the Old Hill Inn, then left down the road to join Philpin Lane on the right. Continue north *(onto map 9)* for Bruntscar, to pick up the route of walk 9 in reverse, climbing straight up for the summit of Whernside. From the summit descend past Force Gill, onto the clear path alongside the railway to Ribblehead Station. *(In bad weather follow Linear Link Route L11 to Ribblehead via Selside.)*

Stage 3: Ribblehead to Garsdale *(Maps 9, 12 & 13)*

11.2 miles (*18.0 km*)   Ascent: 740 m   Time: 5:45 hrs

From Ribblehead the way follows Linear Link Route L9 for Dentdale, turning up Arten Gill to climb Great Knoutberry and along the Coal Road to Garsdale.

(Map 9) Follow the route of Linear Link Walk L9 over Blea Moor *(onto map 12)*, dropping to join the Dent Road at Bridge End. Follow the road north to the bridge at Stone House, turning right to climb up Arten Gill. Where the track begins to level at a junction, go through the gate and follow the wall on the left to a stile which leads to the summit of Great Knoutberry. (*In bad weather, follow the easier alternative drove road round the south-western flank of Knoutberry.*) From the summit head west, descending to join the old drove road, following it right onto the Coal Road. Turn right *(onto map 13)* and follow the quiet road all the way to Garsdale Station.

Stage 4: Garsdale to Kirkby Stephen *(Maps 15, 15b, 16b & 16)*

11.9 miles (*19.2 km*)   Ascent: 630 m   Time: 6:00 hrs

From Garsdale the last stage follows Linear Link Route L15, the spectacular ridge route across Swarth Fell and Wild Boar Fell to Kirkby Stephen.

(Map 15) Follow Linear Link Route L15, heading onto Grizedale Common to pick up the ridge route north-west for Swarth Fell Pike *(onto map 15b)*. Continue on to the summit of Swarth Fell. The route goes on north, dipping to a saddle before climbing to the summit edge of Wild Boar Fell. Continue north along the ridge edge *(onto map 16b)*, past the Nab, to begin the long, steady descent *(onto map 16)*. Finally the track joins the Tommy Road, heading west for a short while (*with the option here, if heading for Kirkby Stephen, to cut off right on a footpath under the railway for Croop House, to pick up the route of Walk 16 in reverse, past Halfpenny House for the town*). Veer north to join the road at Moor End, following it out onto the busy A685 for the station. *(In bad weather follow Linear Link Route L16 in reverse along the High Way.)*

Unique guides to Long Distance walks from Skyware Press:

A Dales High Way

The original guides to a 90 mile walk across the glorious high country of the Yorkshire Dales.

"Promoted through a superbly illustrated Companion book, rich in local geology, history and wildlife, with detailed OS-based maps in an excellent Route Guide, the Dales High Way is a sure-fire winner for all keen Dales walkers,"

- Colin Speakman, Yorkshire Dales Review

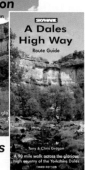

A Dales High Way: Route Guide
A Dales High Way Companion

Tony & Chris Grogan

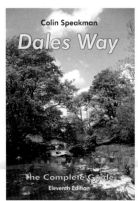

Dales Way

Colin Speakman

The original classic 80 mile trail from Ilkley to Bowness-on-Windermere.

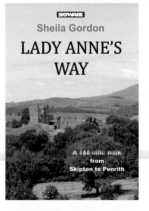

Lady Anne's Way

Sheila Gordon

100 miles following in the footsteps of the remarkable Lady Anne Clifford.

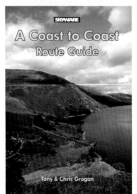

A Coast to Coast Route Guide

Tony & Chris Grogan

Wainwright's classic walk across northern England.

Heart of the Pennine Way

Tony & Chris Grogan

165 miles along the Heart of Britain's premier National Trail.

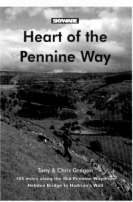